CW00960214

THE FALL OF THE TAY BRIDGE

THE FALL OF THE TAY BRIDGE

David Swinfen

BIRLINN

First published in 1994 by Mercat Press
This second edition published in 2016 by
Birlinn Limited
West Newington House
10 Newington Road
Edinburgh
EH9 1QS

www.birlinn.co.uk

Copyright © David Swinfen 1994, 2016

The moral right of David Swinfen to be identified as the author of
this work has been asserted by him in accordance with the Copyright,
Designs and Patents Act 1988.
All rights reserved. No part of this publication may be
reproduced, stored or transmitted in any form without the express
written permission of the publisher.

ISBN: 978 1 78027 357 0

British Library Cataloguing-in-Publication Data
A catalogue record for this book is available from the British Library

Typeset in ITC Galliard at Birlinn

Printed and bound by
TJ International, Cornwall

CONTENTS

ILLUSTRATIONS

To the memory of William M. Dow, a lifelong Tay Bridge enthusiast

ACKNOWLEDGEMENTS

Historians and historical research are nothing without source material, and that means libraries, especially archival collections. I am extremely grateful to the staffs of the Dundee City Library, the Archives Department of Dundee University, Dundee City Archives, the National Archives of Scotland and the National Library of Scotland. For their expert advice on technical aspects of the Tay Bridge story I have relied heavily on Tom Martin, Professor Iain Macleod of Strathclyde University and Professor Roland Paxton of Heriot-Watt. Professor Paxton also kindly agreed to write the Foreword to this edition.

I should also like to thank my fellow Trustees in the Tay Rail Bridge Disaster Memorial Trust, in particular Murray Nicoll and Ian Nimmo White, for their advice and support, and my editor at Birlinn, Tom Johnstone. It was Tom who saw the first edition of the book through to publication, and now has had to do it all over again.

As always I owe a great debt to my wife Ann, whose dedication to her own work as an historical novelist is a constant inspiration.

FOREWORD

This is an important book because Professor Swinfen, for the first time in a popular text, highlights the findings of Tom Martin and Professor Iain Macleod based on their comprehensive structural assessment published in the *Proceedings of the Institution of Civil Engineers* in 1995 and 2004. Most previous books on the subject have promoted the hypothesis that collapse occurred not primarily from the inherent weakness of the structure to extreme wind force, but from damage caused by the derailed train, or, uncharacteristically for cast iron, fatigue.

When writing history it is important to seek after truth. In a technical context, such as the reason why the Tay Bridge fell, this is best done from an understanding of material properties and the forces at play in its parts under various loading conditions. Previous writers on the Tay Bridge disaster tended not to address these issues in a comprehensive way. Fortunately for public understanding, Professor Swinfen avoids this pitfall and arrives at what deserves to be regarded as the final word in this subject.

Professor Roland Paxton, MBE, FICE, FRSE
Heriot-Watt University

About the Author

David Swinfen was born in Kirkcaldy, Fife, and has lived in Scotland for most of his life – more than half of it within a short distance from the Tay Bridge. He was educated at Kirkcaldy High School and Fettes College, Edinburgh, and served as a platoon commander in a Scottish regiment during the Malayan Emergency, before taking up a scholarship at Hertford College, Oxford, to read Modern History. After graduating with an Honours degree, he embarked on postgraduate study in Imperial history, and was awarded the Beit Prize and Beit Studentship in that subject, gaining a D.Phil degree in 1965.

Employed initially as an Assistant in Modern History at Queen's College, Dundee (later the University of Dundee), he served at various times as Director of American Studies, Head of Modern History, and Dean of the Faculty of Arts and Social Sciences. In 1990 he was appointed to a personal Chair in Commonwealth History, and subsequently to be Vice Principal of the University, a post he held for some ten years before retiring in 2002. Since then he has worked in Sri Lanka for the British Council, and as a Trustee of various Scottish charities. He is currently the chairman of the Tay Rail Bridge Disaster Memorial Trust.

Swinfen's publications include books and articles on Imperial and Commonwealth history, American history, and Scottish history, his most recent being the biography of James Wellwood Moncreiff, a leading nineteenth-century advocate, politician and judge of the Court of Session. He is a Fellow of the Royal Historical Society and the Royal Society of Arts. He lives in Broughty Ferry with his wife Ann, the historical novelist.

INTRODUCTION
to the Revised Edition

The writing of history seldom stands still. Since the first edition of *The Fall of the Tay Bridge* came out in 1994, several more books and articles have been published about the Tay Bridge Disaster, leading to the need to update the original book in two areas in particular. Over the years much attention has been given to the central question of causation – precisely why did the bridge fall? This new edition surveys the substantial literature on this issue, before coming to its own – hopefully authoritative – conclusion. Then there is the equally debatable matter of the number of victims. Most recently this question has been explored by members of the Tay Valley Family History Society, and their conclusions written – literally – in stone, in the form of granite-panelled memorials to the victims. These memorials were erected on both sides of the Tay by the Tay Rail Bridge Disaster Memorial Trust on 28 December, 2013 – the 134th anniversary of the disaster.

At the same time the opportunity has been taken to add substantially to the number of illustrations, many of which have not been published before.

CHAPTER 1

THE BRIDGE IS DOWN

—◆—

At about a quarter past seven on the evening of Sunday 28 December 1879, in one of the worst storms in years, the thirteen central spans – the 'high girders' – of the rail bridge over the Tay between Wormit and Dundee fell into the river, carrying with them the 5.20 train from Burntisland and all the passengers and crew. There were no survivors.[1]

THE STORM GETS UP

Throughout Scotland that weekend south-westerly winds had raged across the country, causing widespread damage, especially to shipping. The Glasgow steamer *Norseman* was washed up on the shore near Portpatrick with no sign of its crew of ten. In the Gairloch, the schooner *Banshee* went down and two other vessels ran aground. On the east coast a number of ships got into difficulties battling against the wind in the Firth of Forth. The schooner *Alma*, bound for Bo'ness with a cargo of pit props, had got as far as Inchkeith before being driven onto a sandbank off Burntisland. The captain of a steamship which arrived at Leith from Gothenburg swore he had never known such a storm in all his years at sea, and that he had had to lash two helmsmen to the wheel for their own safety.[2]

Yet on the Sunday morning the wind moderated slightly. The ferry from Granton to Burntisland, carrying passengers from Edinburgh to join the train for Dundee via the new rail bridge over the Tay estuary, continued to run normally. In Dundee there had been little indication earlier in the day of the disaster to come. The weather that morning had been fine, and conditions for the ferry crossing over the Tay continued to be relatively smooth until well into the afternoon. When dusk fell, not long after 4.00 p.m., the wind had freshened slightly, and an hour later, the captain of the ferry reported the river 'was getting up very fast'. By six, when the ferry docked again on the Dundee side, all the signs were that a violent storm was imminent.[3]

Dundee had its share of weather watchers, both amateur and professional. Amongst them was Admiral Dougall, long retired now, but still meticulous in his observations of weather conditions from his house at Scotscraig on the Fife side of the river. Unlike most observers, the Admiral had felt uneasy about the weather earlier in the day. By four o'clock the rain was heavy, and his barometer showed a fall from 29.40 to 28.80. In the Admiral's garden the trees and bushes were being battered by the force of the rain, and he became concerned about his old walnut tree, and whether it would survive the force of a high wind. Looking out towards the open sea, he noted how the wind came in sudden fierce gusts, which he estimated at between 75 and 78 miles per hour.[4]

Out on the river lay the *Mars* training ship, home for the past ten years of young Dundee lads destined for a life on the sea, or in the city's bustling textile mills. Its captain, Captain Scott, had also been keeping an eye on the glass, and had noted the sudden fall in pressure in the later afternoon. As the wind reached its height, he reckoned the gale to be between 10 and 11 on the Beaufort scale – the worst gale he could remember on the Tay for the past six years. In Fife an engineer called Brodie had travelled over the bridge to his home in Cupar on the day before the disaster, but was forbidden to return the next day by his father, a strict Sabbatarian. In the middle of the night he was woken by water pouring into his house, and discovered that the flat lead sheet covering the roof, and weighing more than a ton, had been rolled up by the wind.[5]

On the Dundee side, in a house overlooking Magdalen Green with a clear view of both river and bridge, retired businessman Charles Clark had been keeping a log of the weather for the past fourteen years. Like the others he had noted the fall in barometric pressure and, using a scale of his own from 1 to 6, recorded the force of the wind at the maximum of the scale.

Just before six o'clock the harbourmaster, William Robertson, called into his office, and left again at five minutes past. He had 'some little difficulty', he said later, 'in turning the corner at the tidal basin', and after he had reached the west end of the Customs House he found himself caught by the full force of the gale. When he eventually managed to reach his home nearby, he told his wife that the weather was too bad for her to venture out to evening service, and he set out on his own.[6]

By this time the wind was starting to cause some damage. Throughout the city slates were torn off roofs, and chimney pots smashed to the ground. The wind whipped through a line of bathing huts on the shore below the esplanade, near the northern landfall of the bridge, ripping off their roofs and dashing them against the wall. Down at Taybridge Station the wind blew three loaded coal wagons 400 yards along a siding, and the engine-shed foreman, James Roberts, set his men to barricade the doors of the shed. At about six o'clock he decided to call the stationmaster, and set off for his house.[7]

Within the station itself the devastation was considerable. Taybridge Station then, as now, lay parallel to the river in an east-west direction. To the east, the line ran into a tunnel before sloping up into the area of the docks. To the west, the station was open to the wind, which by this time had moved round so that it blew almost directly along the station platforms. Its escape effectively blocked at the eastern end, the gale took the line of least resistance, which happened to be the glass roof covering most of the station. By the time he arrived at his office, James Smith found the whole station a wilderness of broken glass, and at once ordered it to be closed to the public.[8]

Also in the station were the crew from the local from Newport, waiting to take their train back again across the Bridge. They had left Newport at 5.50, just as the gale was getting up, with two employees of the Caledonian Railway in the van with the guard, Robert Shand. As the train gathered speed on the bridge, they could feel the van heeling over under the force of the wind, and the howl of the gale was deafening. One of the Caledonian men, John Buick, looked out of the window and saw showers of sparks coming from the wheels of the train. He shouted out, 'Shand, there is something wrong with the train!', but Shand took little notice, since he knew from experience that the sparks were caused by the friction of the wheel flanges against the rails, under the force of the wind. He did, however, take the precaution of giving the brake handle a few twists, and waving a red lantern out of the window, in the hope that the driver, Alexander Kennedy, would see it and slow down. Kennedy saw nothing, but he did feel the drag of the brake. As he told friends later, 'I just let her out a bit more'.[9]

THE 'EDINBURGH'

By the time that Kennedy, Shand and the others arrived in Dundee, the next train to cross the bridge, or rather to fail to do so, was already well on its way across Fife. Although this train began its journey at Burntisland, on the Fife shore of the Firth of Forth, it was known among railwaymen as the 'Edinburgh', since it provided the last link in a long and wearisome trek for travellers making their way from Scotland's capital to Dundee. The first stage would have been by the 4.15 train from Waverley Station in Edinburgh to Granton, on the southern shore of the Firth; then by way of the passenger ferry across the estuary to Burntisland, where a second train would have been waiting. This second train was due to leave at 5.27, stopping at no fewer than 14 intermediate stations on the way, and was expected to arrive at Dundee's Taybridge Station at about 7.15 p.m.

On this particular Sunday, the 'Edinburgh' was made up of five passenger coaches and the guard's van. The engine, No. 224, driven by David Mitchell, was a replacement for the Drummond tank engine which normally pulled the train, but which was being repaired. No. 224 had been built in Cowlairs in 1871, one of the first of the standard British 4-4-0 type. She was equipped with a Westinghouse brake, and was painted smartly in olive green with brightly polished brass trim. Next to the engine came the first of the three first-class carriages, a four-wheeler weighing eight and a half tons, then a six-wheeled first-class carriage weighing fourteen and a quarter, two more third-class coaches, and after them the only second-class coach, much smaller and lighter than the rest. At the rear came the van, carrying David Macbeath, the guard, and 46 mailbags.[10]

Apparently so far unaffected by the storm, the 'Edinburgh' made remarkably good time across Fife. Only slightly late at Thornton Junction, the train got to Leuchars, about four miles short of the bridge, at around 7 o'clock. Although in those days a rail link existed, there were no trains from St Andrews to Leuchars on a Sunday. However, one fortunate passenger, a Mr Linskill, had made arrangements for a coach to meet him at Leuchars Station and take him on to St Andrews by road. At first there was no sign of the coach, and Linskill had got back on to the train intending to find overnight lodgings in Dundee, when at the very last minute, just as the train was about to set off again, a light on the road was seen, the coach appeared, and he was able to get down and complete his homeward journey.[11]

There was still one final stop before the bridge – at St Fort Station, where all the tickets for Dundee passengers were collected, and those for passengers for further destinations were examined. As the storm raged, the stationmaster and the porter hurried to help the ticket collector get the job done quickly, noticing, as they bustled through the train, that there seemed to be an unusually large number of passengers for a Sunday, due no doubt to the closeness to the New Year holiday. Amongst the passengers they noticed some of their fellow employees on the North British staff, including George Ness, an engine cleaner who had recently passed the examination for promotion to fireman, and who was married to the daughter of John Brand, one of the engine drivers on the line.[12]

Most of the other passengers also came from the locality. One of them was Ann Cruickshank, a spinster in her early fifties, and housemaid to Lady Baxter of Kilmaron. Ann's body would be the first to be found after the disaster. There was William Threlfall, a shop assistant from Dundee, returning after visiting his soldier brothers in Edinburgh; John Scott, a sailor, recently discharged from his ship and almost home again; Walter Ness, a Dundee saddler, back from visiting friends at Auchtermuchty; William Macdonald, a sawmiller from Blackness Road, travelling with his eleven-year-old son Davie, after a visit to friends in Fife; William Jack, a grocer; James Crichton, a ploughman; William Peebles, a forester; and many more. There were one or two more women – Jessie Bain, with her brother Archie, a farmer; and Eliza Scott travelling with her sweetheart George Johnston, who had joined the train at St Fort to be with her on the short trip to Dundee. There was an Englishman, William Henry Beynon, a photographer from Cheltenham, up in Scotland on a business trip.[13]

Stationmaster Morris and his companions closed the doors and stood back as the 'Edinburgh' set off once more. At the approach to the bridge the train paused but did not stop as the fireman, John Marshall, leant out of the cab to snatch the bridge baton, which gave his train the right of way on the single track bridge, from the hand of signalman Thomas Barclay. Gathering speed, it passed over the first section of spans – the 'low girders' – before battling its way onto the first of the 'high girders', eighty-eight feet above the navigable channel, through whose latticework sides the wind whistled and shrieked. At some point in its passage through this part of the bridge the train was attacked by a gust of appalling ferocity. Train, bridge, passengers, crew – all fell

5

headlong down into the black waters of the Tay frothing and swirling beneath them.[14]

Who Saw It Fall?

Few could say with certainty that they were witnesses to its fall. It was a Sunday and a storm was blowing. Most of the citizens were at home around their firesides or, like harbourmaster Robertson, at evening service in church. There were some, however, whose houses overlooked the river, and who for one reason or another were watching out for the train as it crossed the bridge. At the home of George Clark, wine merchant, a hundred yards or so from the signal box at the north end of the bridge, George and his brother William stood in adjacent rooms and waited for a glimpse of the train. George had travelled in the Far East and had experience of hurricanes on the China seas. He could see the lights of the train flickering as it entered the latticework sides of the high girders, and at that crucial moment he turned his head away. In the next room William kept his eyes firmly on the train, and as it reached the third pier of the high girders, so he said afterwards, three flashes of light came in quick succession, seeming to fall obliquely into the river. 'Look at the fire!' called William, 'the train is over the bridge!'[15]

A little further along Magdalen Green, from an upstairs room, young Alexander Maxwell and his friend William Millar watched for the train, and a little after seven o'clock they saw its lights appear dimly at the other end of the bridge. As it entered the high girders they both saw the three flashes, though Alexander thought they came from in front of the train, while William was sure they came from the train itself. He called out that the bridge was down, though no-one would believe him until Alexander's father had gone to get his telescope, to see for himself the great gap in the bridge and the broken stumps of the iron supporting columns against which the waves thrashed.[16]

In a snug little house within sight of the bridge a father was reading a bible story to his children – appropriately enough the story of St Paul's shipwreck on the island of Melita – when the 'thundering crash' of a falling chimney pot brought them all to the window. As the father himself retailed it to the *Dundee Advertiser*, in the moonlight, as it shone through gaps in the clouds, they could just make out the bridge with the train moving along it. Suddenly one of the children exclaimed, 'that's just like lightning!', and sure enough 'a comet-like burst of fiery sparks burst from the engine, and the streak of fire was seen till quenched in the stormy water below. Then there was absolute darkness on the bridge. A silence fell upon the eager group at the window. Then with stunning force the idea broke upon my mind. "Heavens!" I cried, "I fear the train is over the bridge!"'[17]

Some watchers were out in the storm when the bridge fell. Not far from the house of George Clark, but a little over to the west lived James Lawson. A few minutes after seven o'clock he decided to go out and see what effect the storm might have had on the structure, and as he battled his way towards it he happened upon a friend of his called Smart. Together they watched as the train came slowly towards them. Suddenly the train lights disappeared, and a ball of fire fell down into the water. 'There is the train in the river!' shouted Smart, and the two of them ran for shelter under one of the northern spans.[18]

Up in Blackness Road lived Peter Barron, a carriage inspector with the Caledonian Railway. At 7.00 he heard the sound of a chimney pot falling and went outside to investigate. Looking across to the bridge he could just make out the lights of the train as it crept along towards the high girders, when it seemed to him that part of the bridge fell away, and then another part, while at the same time a light appeared in the river. A gap in the clouds appeared and the moon shone through briefly – just long enough for him to make out the empty space where the high girders had been.[19]

Out on the training ship *Mars*, which lay directly downstream from the bridge, the deck watch should have been in the best position of all to see what really happened. Like the others, he had watched as the train went out onto the bridge, and had seen the lights flicker as the train entered the high girders, but at that very moment a great gust of wind caught the ship and made him turn away for cover. When he could look up again the lights had disappeared, and so had the central spans of the bridge. He sounded the alarm.[20]

Out at Magdalen Point James Lawson met up with George Clark, who had left his house to get a closer look at the bridge, and together they ran to the north signal box to see if there was any word of the train. Climbing up the steps of the box they met signalman Henry Somerville on the way down. 'Where is the train?' they asked. 'It's been a long time on the bridge,' Somerville replied. Not satisfied, Lawson and Clark ran to the station.

At Taybridge Station itself, stationmaster James Smith was getting increasingly worried at the non-arrival of the train. The position of the signals showed that it must have passed the signal box at the south end of the bridge, but the minutes slipped by with no sign of it. Although there was no telegraph operator on duty on a Sunday, Robert Shand, the guard from the local, tried to get through to the south box, but without success. At that point they were hailed by Clark and Lawson, who told them that the train had gone down into the river. Not yet convinced – the train could conceivably have stopped and retreated to the Fife side – Smith nevertheless ordered his staff to clear the station and close the gates. Together with James Roberts, the engine shed supervisor, he set off to the north box to hear what Somerville had to say. He found little comfort there. According to Somerville he had received a telegraph from Thomas Barclay in the south box at 7.14 to notify him that the train had entered the bridge. Normally it would have taken the train about five minutes to reach his box, and he had gone down to collect the baton in the usual way. The five minutes passed with no sign of it, and at 23 minutes past seven he had climbed back up the steps of the box to peer across the river into the blackness, but there was nothing to be seen. He had tried in vain to get through to the south side by both telegraph and telephone.

Finally Smith and Roberts decided that there was nothing else for it but for them to walk along the bridge and see the damage for themselves. The going was not too difficult to begin with, but soon the wind forced then down on their knees and Smith was overcome with giddiness and could go no further. Bravely, Roberts kept on going, having to crawl now as the wind threatened to tear him from the floor of the bridge, and send him to join the train in the river below. For over half a mile he inched his way along until he reached the end of the low girders – and the end of what was left of the bridge. A few yards ahead of him he could make out the broken ends of the rails pointing down at an angle towards the river, and the shattered end of the water pipe which had carried the supply across the river to Newport, but now gushed uselessly into mid-air. Roberts wasted no more time, but turned and fought his way back to where the others were waiting for him.[21]

There were fewer witnesses on the Fife side of the river. From a window of his house in Newport, former Provost Robertson watched for the train, believing that his son might be on it. He could follow its progress as far as the beginning of the high girders, before it

Engine-shed supervisor James Roberts battles his way to the end of the low girders. *Illustrated London News, Eduardo Alessandro Gallery*

disappeared behind a house and was lost to view. He never saw it reappear, but instead made out two distinct columns of spray rise high above the bridge and then, so it seemed, the navigation lights of the bridge fell away towards the water.[22]

In the south signal box, Thomas Barclay had telegraphed to Somerville that the train was on its way, set the signals to allow it on

9

to the bridge, and gone down to the track to hand the baton to John Marshall on the engine footplate. He had then climbed back into the box to join his friend John Watt, an off-duty employee of the railway, who had come out with Barclay to keep him company on the stormy night. Watt kept his eyes on the train as it drew away from them along the bridge, able to see both the three red lights fixed to the back of the guard's van, and the shower of sparks from the wheels as they rubbed against the rail. A sudden flash from the high girders distracted his attention, and when he looked again, the red lights had gone. 'Something has happened to the train', he told Barclay, but Barclay reassured him – the train had simply gone over the hump in the middle of the bridge, as it always did.

But of course there was nothing normal about the train on this particular night. The expected signal from Somerville to acknowledge its arrival at the north box never came – indeed they soon found that all telegraph and telephone connections with the north shore had gone dead. Like Smith and Roberts, Barclay and Watt decided to try to see what had gone wrong for themselves, but could only struggle a little way along the bridge before the wind defeated them and they had to turn back. While Barclay stuck to his post in the signal box, Watt set off for the nearby station of St Fort, but finding that the stationmaster at St Fort was out, decided to battle on the four miles to Leuchars. By the time he got there he was in such a distressed state that Thomas Robertson the stationmaster refused to believe his story and sent for a doctor. At last convinced that Watt was telling the truth, Robertson set off in the doctor's gig for St Andrews, where the tragic news was confirmed by telegraph, whereupon he turned around and went back to Leuchars.[23]

A Boat Goes out

Back in Dundee, harbourmaster Robertson (Robertson is still one of the most common surnames in Dundee today) had come out of church at about eight o'clock. The service had been held against a background of the roar of the storm, and at 7.15 the minister had been obliged to pause in his address as his words were drowned by a huge gust of wind and a loud tearing noise from the roof. Out in the street there were slates and broken chimney pots scattered all around, and an anxious crowd who had heard the rumour that the bridge was down.

Robertson hurried first to the station, but Smith and Roberts were still out on the bridge, so he made for his own office at the harbour and stared incredulously at what remained of the bridge through the office telescope.[24]

Certainly a boat should go out, but no boat was immediately available. The harbour tug was beached, and could not be refloated until the next tide in five hours' time, while the ferry *Dundee*, having been stormbound since six o'clock, had only just left for Newport. In the meantime, while Robertson waited for the return of the ferry in an agony of impatience, at Taybridge Station two men had arrived in response to a message from the stationmaster – Provost Brownlie and Mr James Cox, a prominent Dundee industrialist and chairman of the Tay Bridge Undertaking, which had raised the capital for building the bridge. Their first thoughts seem to have been to prevent a panic by letting out as little information as possible. Local newspaperman John Malloch described how, after they had arrived at the station:

> Great care was taken that no-one who had come to meet friends should learn of the fears of the railway authorities, and at length they were advised to go home in the belief that the railway authorities perhaps thought it dangerous to allow trains on the bridge, and that probably it was being kept back until the gale moderated.[25]

Such attempts to supress information about the real state of affairs were futile. From the central post office of the town there arrived Mr Gibb, the Postmaster, with more distressing news. He had received a telegram from the postmistress of Broughty Ferry, a few miles down the estuary, to say that mailbags had been washed ashore there on the beach. There could be no clearer confirmation of the fate of the train.

At long last the *Dundee* reappeared, with Captain Methven, the ferry superintendent, aboard. It was now ten o'clock, more than two and a half hours since the bridge had gone down, but conditions on the water had forced the ferry to make a long detour, and she had been unable even to approach the bridge. While there could be little hope now of finding any survivors, nevertheless the ferry was quickly supplied with blankets and 'medical comforts', and with the harbourmaster, the Provost, the stationmaster, a doctor, and various other gentlemen on board, set off for the bridge. Captain Methven took her in as close as he dared, before lowering a boat which the crew rowed from one end of the gap to the other, through water littered with planks ripped from the floor of the bridge. They could see clearly that all the high girders were down, and the iron columns which had supported them were broken off, leaving only the stumps of the piers sticking forlornly out of the water, as they still do today. But of the people who had been aboard the Edinburgh, there was no sign at all.[26]

THE 'SPECIAL' FROM EDINBURGH

It was time to alert others to the catastrophe. Station master James Smith sent off the following telegram via the Caledonian Railway line to a Mr Bell at the North British Railway Company's office at Portobello:

'TERRIBLE ACCIDENT ON BRIDGE. ONE OR MORE OF HIGH GIRDERS BLOWN DOWN. AM NOT SURE AS TO SAFETY OF LAST TRAIN DOWN FROM EDIN-BURGH. WILL ADVISE FURTHER AS SOON AS CAN BE OBTAINED.' [sic][27]

The message was soon relayed to the Chairman of the Company, John Stirling, who in turn got word to the bridge's designer, Sir Thomas Bouch, at his home in Edinburgh. Arrangements were made for both of them, together with John Walker, the general manager, to travel by special train to Dundee, necessarily following the same route as the ill-fated Edinburgh, at least as far as the south shore of the Firth of Tay. They left Edinburgh on the special at 12.20 a.m. on the Monday morning, and having arrived at Granton, crossed the Forth on *Leviathan*, the special rail ferry designed according to Bouch's own plan to carry goods wagons across the river to Burntisland, and then on by train again, arriving at Leuchars at 4.00 a.m., where stationmaster Thomas Robertson was ready to greet them. Bouch, Robertson reported later, 'was in a pitiful state of mind'.

At Leuchars the principals were given the latest information, including a report from stationmaster Morris from St Fort, in which he estimated, quite wrongly as it turned out, that the train had been carrying some 300 passengers when it went down. This mistake may have arisen from a count having been made of all the tickets collected at St Fort Station that day, instead of for the tickets for the 'Edinburgh' alone. In actual fact there could not have been room on the train for as many as 300 passengers, and later estimates put the number on the train at 75, though only 46 bodies were ever recovered. The most recent research, based both on the official police report and the death certificates preserved in the National Register of Archives in Edinburgh, suggests that the true figure of those who are known to have been lost was 59.[28] Most unfortunately the figure of 300 was included in John Walker's report which he telegraphed from Leuchars to the North British office in Edinburgh shortly after his arrival:

> From the reports made to us here of the terrible calamity at the Tay Bridge it appears that several of the large girders of the bridge along with the last train from Edinburgh were precipitated into the river about half past seven last night. There were, I deeply deplore to say, nearly 300 passengers besides the Company's servants on the train, all of whom are believed to have perished. The cause of the accident has not yet been ascertained.[29]

Chapter 2

RAILWAY RIVALRY

⋙◆⋘

Railway Mania

The 1840s in Britain had been a decade of extraordinary expansion of the nation's rail network. Speculators rushed to Parliament with their plans for railway construction (for the law required that each new line be the subject of its own special Parliamentary Bill), and engineers were kept busy providing plans for the promoters, many of whose schemes would never be put into practical effect. By the early years of the next decade, the broad outlines of the network were visibly in place. All the main cities of England were joined together by thin ribbons of iron, and the great days when fortunes were made from railway promotion were almost over. Yet 'railway mania' persisted, if at a less frantic level. Companies continued to be formed to join lesser towns to the main arterial lines by branches and spurs. There was little attempt by the promoters, and not much by Parliament, to develop these lines according to some well thought-out national strategy, and the combination of a lack of strategic planning and an excessive haste to realise elusive profits resulted in the development of lines which might never manage to pay their way. Inevitably these trends led to cut-throat competition between railway companies, and this in turn led either to the collapse of some companies, or to the merger of two or more companies together.

The Scottish Railways

In Scotland the situation was in some ways even worse than in England. The main Scottish companies, like their English counterparts the product of the glittering years of the mania, were mostly managed by men who had a real talent for promoting their lines and getting them built, but rather less for the day to day running of a rail system. 'There is something wrong about the management of

14

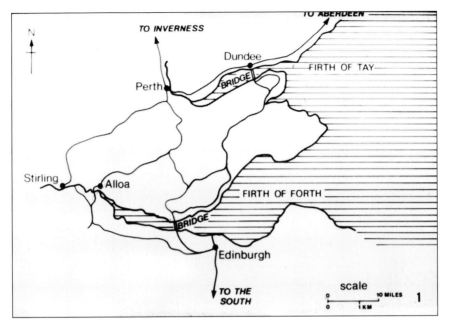

Railway routes in the east coast of Scotland, showing the Tay and Forth bridges. *Victor Bignell*

Scottish railways,' commented a railway journal of the day, 'notwithstanding the national character of that country for economy. But [in railway business] we find them to be comparatively extravagant in large matters, penurious in little, lax, and unsuccessful'.[30] Amongst the particular weaknesses of Scottish railway management was failure to estimate accurately the costs involved in setting up a railway in the first place. In 1852 the *Railway Times*, writing about the Edinburgh, Perth and Dundee line, complained that 'experience has shown that no railway contract is ever completed for the price for which it is undertaken . . . The eagerness to embark in railways, as well as the inexperience of the difficulties and uncertainties attendant on them, appear to have alike deceived projectors, engineers and subscribers'.[31] Thus the Caledonian Railway, which had allowed £173.000 for the purchase of land on which to build the line, ended up by paying nearly £390,000, while the North British, the Aberdeen, and the Edinburgh and Northern all paid out three times their original estimates. Huge sums also were expended on the Parliamentary and legal costs connected with getting the necessary legislation through, without which no work on building the line could even begin.

15

When it came to the actual operation of the lines, a series of enquiries into the Scottish companies revealed extraordinary stories of extravagance and financial irresponsibility – themselves born of the ruinous competition for routes between the major players in the business. On the one hand, companies committed themselves to guarantees to the shareholders of lines which they had leased, largely to prevent their rivals getting control of what they regarded as their territory, while on the other (and for the same reasons) they engaged in disastrous price-cutting exercises, making it impossible for those guarantees to be honoured. In the second half of 1850 four of the leading Scottish rail companies, the Caledonian, the North British, the Scottish Central, and the Edinburgh, Perth and Dundee, all failed to pay a dividend to their shareholders.[32]

The 1850s and 1860s in Scotland saw an increasingly bitter battle being fought out between the major companies for a position of dominance in the railway business, and as time went on that battle developed into a contest principally between two giants – the Caledonian and the North British. The North British Railway Company had originated in 1846 as a relatively small concern, operating the line southward from Edinburgh to Berwick-upon-Tweed, but from these small beginnings had developed a growing empire of branch lines between the capital and the borders. In August 1862, under the control of expansionist chairman Richard Hodgson, the company took two important steps towards the major league – it inaugurated the new Waverley route from Edinburgh to Carlisle, and on the very same day took over the Edinburgh, Perth and Dundee line, giving it control over the whole of the east coast route from Berwick to Dundee. More than that – the takeover of the Edinburgh, Perth and Dundee line would enable the North British to outflank the Caledonian, and develop an east coast network, at the heart of which was a line from Edinburgh to Dundee some 28 miles shorter than the Caledonian route.[33]

Over much the same time-span, the Caledonian had also been advancing on Dundee, but from the starting point of Carlisle, moving northward until it met with the southern end of the Scottish Central at Greenhill. In 1863 the Scottish Central took over the Dundee, Perth and Aberdeen Railway Junction Company, thus gaining direct access to Dundee, while from Dundee northward, the Scottish North Eastern Railway took the line as far as Aberdeen. As the Caledonian had negotiated an arrangement with both the Scottish Central and the Scottish

North Eastern to have use of their lines, by 1863 the Caledonian effectively controlled the whole central route from Carlisle to Aberdeen, and within a further three years had consolidated its position by taking over both of the smaller lines. Thus, by the mid-sixties the Caledonian and the North British stood face to face across the Tay, ready for the final battle for supremacy. Which of them would emerge the victor would depend crucially on the building of the bridge over the Tay.[34]

There was of course a serious snag, or rather two – the two great firths of Forth and Tay, which separated the Kingdom of Fife from Lothian to the south and Angus to the North. So long as these huge natural obstacles remained unbridged, the advantage to the North British of having the shorter route remained academic. The dream of overcoming these obstacles had long been the great ambition of one of the central figures in the Tay Bridge tragedy – the engineer Thomas Bouch.

THOMAS BOUCH

Thomas Bouch was the third son of William Bouch, a retired captain in the merchant navy, and was born in the small village of Thursby in Cumberland in 1822. His interest in engineering as a career was first aroused, we are told, by a lecture on hydraulics given by the village schoolmaster, Joseph Hannah, and when Hannah moved to the headship of a school in Carlisle, young Thomas went with him to complete his education. After a brief and unsatisfactory period of employment in an engineering works in Liverpool, Bouch returned to Carlisle, where he was taken on by a local civil engineer called Larmer, who was currently engaged on the Lancaster and Carlisle railway. Bouch stayed with Larmer for about four years, went for a short time to Leeds, and then spent a further four years as resident engineer with the Stockton and Darlington railway. In 1849 he moved again, this time to become both manager and engineer of what was then the Edinburgh and Northern Railway, later known as the Edinburgh, Perth and Dundee, a line which, as we have seen, was ultimately absorbed by the North British in 1862.[35]

THE 'FLOATING RAILWAY'

It was during his time at the Edinburgh and Northern that Bouch first confronted the problem caused by the wide estuaries of the Forth and

Sir Thomas Bouch, 1822–80, designer of the ill-fated first Tay Bridge.
Dundee University Archives

Tay rivers. His solution to it was both ingenious and effective – not the construction of a bridge, which would have been quite beyond the means of the Company at that time, but the provision of what became known as a 'floating railway' – in fact a specially designed ferry boat with rails on the deck, on to which goods wagons were manoeuvred by means of a movable ramp on the quay. The vessel was designed by Thomas Grainger, the engineer who had built the line in the first place, while Bouch himself designed the ramp mechanism.[36]

One of the many obituaries of Bouch published on his death in 1880 gives full details of this simple but ingenious device:

> The invention embraced three principal features – the inclined plane, the flying bridge connecting the moveable framework with the ship's deck, and the means adopted to secure free space for the shipment of trucks on board. Upon a massive inclined plane of masonry, the moveable framework runs on sixteen wheels, the upper part of the frame presenting two lines of rails on the level, while below the beams and fillings take on the form of a slope. This framework is pulled up or down on the ship to suit the state of the tide. At its centre rise two uprights, with a crossbeam, the uprights sustaining heavy weights with chains over pulleys, and thence to strong cranes or jibs which, hinged at the outer end of the framework, support girders that stretch forward to meet the vessel. These hinged girders allow for the play of the vessel and for the rise and fall of the tide while loading and unloading go on. On board the vessel the difficulty arose that, as paddle wheels must be used to give breadth and stability for the rough crossing, the shaft would interfere with the clear run fore and aft. This difficulty was overcome by providing for each paddle a separate engine, with the result that on the several lines of rails trucks can be at once run on board over the whole deck space. The first cargo carried across the Forth by the vessel consisted of four hundred tons of turnips.[37]

There were of course already ferries in operation across both rivers when Bouch joined the Edinburgh and Northern, but the service they provided was slow, unreliable and expensive. On each river the company operated two boats for freight and one for passengers, but

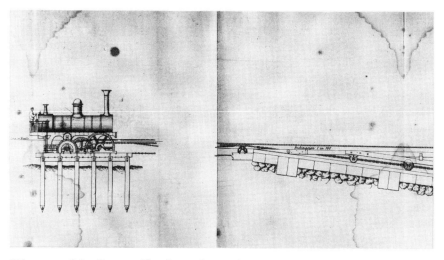

Diagram of the famous 'floating railway' designed by Thomas Bouch to carry goods trains across the Forth and Tay estuaries. *Dundee University Archives*

The floating railway at Broughty Harbour, with the train pulling away.

Model of the floating railway in Broughty Castle Museum.
Dundee City Council (Dundee Art Galleries and Museums)

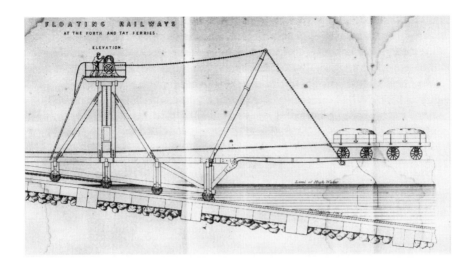

goods brought to the ferry terminal had first to be unloaded from wagons to boat and then loaded on to wagons again at the other side – a process which had to be repeated at the next crossing. Not only was this time-consuming, but the cost per mile to operate the ferries was a massive six times the operating cost of rail. Moreover the inefficiency of the system denied to the line the lucrative business of transporting very large loads. The great advantage of the floating railway was that it cut out the loading and unloading process – goods wagons were run directly on and off the boat.

Bouch was successful in persuading the company to go ahead with his scheme, and an order was placed for the first of the ferries – the *Leviathan* – with Napiers of Glasgow. The new boat was delivered to Granton in September 1849. On the 11th of that month Bouch wrote to the chairman:

> The large steamer for conveying animals and merchandise across the [Tay] ferry was thought better adapted for the Forth, and has accordingly been sent there. A similar one in its stead is being built to effect the same object by Mr Napier of Glasgow and will be ready and on the passage by January next. By that time the necessary apparatus for running the wagons on and off board will be finished so as to enable you to send your goods and minerals into Dundee and Arbroath without change of truck.[38]

In fact it took longer than Bouch had planned to install the machinery, and *Leviathan* did not begin her work of transporting freight across the Forth until March of the following year. In operation *Leviathan* could carry up to 34 goods wagons, while the average time for a crossing, including loading and unloading, was just under an hour. Her counterpart on the Tay, the *Robert Napier*, was introduced in 1851, where with her sister ship the *Carrier* she ran from Tayport to Broughty Ferry until the opening of the bridge in 1878, and again from the fall of the bridge until the new bridge was completed in 1887. In March 1851 Bouch was able to report with some satisfaction on the 'complete success of the floating railway used in the ferry. The steamer and apparatus have been at work thirteen months without so much as one single working day having passed without the conveyance of trucks safely across the firth.' More than 29,000 wagons had been carried over the Forth by the rail ferry in the first six months of operation.[39]

THE BELAH VIADUCT

Shortly after this, and with his reputation in the profession firmly established, Bouch left the Company to set up as an independent consultant, and embarked on a long and successful career as the designer chiefly of cheap rail lines for small companies in the north of England and south-east Scotland. In this capacity he built some 300 miles of railway, though his most extensive single project, for the South Durham and Lancashire Union Railway, was only 50 miles long, and the average length of his lines was only about 15 miles. He also built a number of viaducts to carry his lines across the rough country of the north of England. These included the Hownes Gill Viaduct spanning a deep ravine on the Darlington and Blackhill line, 700 feet long and 175 feet high at its highest point, the Redheugh Viaduct at Newcastle-upon-Tyne, and the Deepdale Viaduct carrying the Barnard Castle and Kirkby Stephen line over Deepdale Beck.[40]

Of his viaducts the best known and certainly the largest was Belah Viaduct, built for the North Eastern Railway over the little Belah river, to enable a line to be carried westward from Barnard Castle over the Pennines into Cumberland and Westmorland. Bouch's plan called for the construction of a viaduct 1,010 feet long, carrying a double track, and with piers ranging from 60 to 100 feet in height, supporting 16 spans of 60 feet each. Two features of this viaduct (still standing more

The Belah Viaduct. *Tom Martin*

than one hundred years later, when it fell victim not to physical decay, but to Dr Beeching's axe) connect it directly with the later ill-fated bridge over the Tay. In the first place the designs of the two bridges were similar, in that both of them made use of piers made up of hollow cast-iron columns braced together, these piers supporting latticework girders – a mode of construction which was simple, cheap, and offered only slight resistance to the wind at high elevations. In the case of the Belah Viaduct, Bouch's employers had instructed him to draw up plans for both cast-iron and stone piers, but soon found that the cast-iron alternative would cost very much less both in time and materials. Secondly, the construction work was carried out by the Middlesbrough firm of Gilkes, Wilson and Co., who as Hopkins, Gilkes and Co., were also the principal contractors for the Tay Bridge. This collaboration was extremely successful – the viaduct was completed in only four months, using an ingenious technique which did away with the need for expensive scaffolding. The total cost of the project was only £31,630, and it was completed without a single injury or accident at any stage – an almost unique record.[41] Moreover the Board of Trade inspector found the whole construction perfectly safe at the first inspection. The contractors' achievement was commemorated in the following verse:

> To future ages these lines will tell
> Who built this structure o'er the dell,
> Gilkes Wilson with his eighty men
> Raised Belah viaduct o'er the glen[42]

THE ST ANDREWS LINE[43]

Bouch also became increasingly involved in railway construction in Scotland. The new managers of Scotland's railways, who in many cases had supplanted the old guard by the mid-1850s, had come to the conclusion that the answer to the low earning potential of railways in thinly populated areas of the country was to cut down on construction costs. New lines could only be built economically where the local landowners were prepared to co-operate and make land available cheaply, where there was no opposition which could make the passage of the proposal through Parliament impossibly expensive, and where there was no need to build to the high specifications of the main line routes. One of the pioneers in Scotland of the movement to build cheap and unassuming lines was the St Andrews Railway Company, which employed Thomas Bouch as its engineer.

The St Andrews Company was well placed to carry out its objective of linking the town with the Edinburgh, Perth and Dundee line at Leuchars. The land in between was flat, no large earthworks were required, and only two small bridges would have to be built. Most of the landowners over whose land the projected line would pass had a financial interest in the scheme, and the Edinburgh, Perth and Dundee itself was happy to co-operate. In no position to build the line with its own financial resources, the company came to an agreement with the promoters to operate and maintain the line for twenty-five years after its opening. They also supplied the St Andrews Company with Bouch as the engineer, who submitted his estimates in August 1850, while still employed by the Edinburgh, Perth and Dundee as manager and resident engineer. Although he resigned in the spring of 1851 to become an independent consultant, he retained the St Andrews Company as his clients, and designed the line for them for a fee of £100 per mile which, so he claimed, was about one fifth of the average engineering fees in

Scotland at the time. He also took special care to reduce the cost of actual construction by 'every economy consistent with obtaining actual safety'. This included specifying lightweight rails, and sleepers spaced four feet apart instead of the usual three. 'With this slight road,' he wrote, 'it was arranged that light engines only should be used, and run at moderate speed.'[44]

It was with the St Andrews commission, then, that Bouch first established himself as a specialist in the construction of cheap, light railway lines, catering to the needs of companies with more enthusiasm than cash. His reputation 'for contriving economical works' carried him to other similar projects in Scotland and in England – the Leven, the Peebles, the Leslie, Crieff Junction, the Eden Valley, the viaducts already mentioned – and altogether he had completed some eighteen or nineteen rail constructions before embarking on what was to be the crowning achievement of his career – the conquest of the firths of Forth and Tay.

The Plan for a Tay Bridge

The idea of constructing an iron bridge across the Tay was not new. As early as 1818 a gentleman of Dundee had expressed a wish that someone might construct a bridge which would join Magdalen Yard Point to Woodhaven, 'which would secure a safe easy and expeditious passage to and from y opposite county, without let or hindrance fr. either squally weather or sandbanks'.[45] From time to time thereafter the idea was mooted, but with no practical result. Bouch himself had first put forward his plan for a bridge over the Tay in 1854, when still in the employ of the Edinburgh, Perth and Dundee company, only for the proposal to be rejected and himself 'looked upon as a dreamer, and treated with an incredulity which was strangely inconsistent with the character of an astute businessman, whose knowledge of what engineers had already accomplished ought to have given them some conception of what man may command in his conflict with Nature.'[46] For the next decade the bridge plan lay dormant, but the acquisition of the Edinburgh, Perth and Dundee Company by the North British in 1862 reopened the whole question of bridging both Forth and Tay, and chairman Richard Hodgson decided to give his backing to the scheme.

Initially the North British plan focussed on the Forth, and Bouch was commissioned to produce a plan for a Forth Bridge which would

Bouch's design for the Forth Bridge.

span the river between Blackness Point on the south side and Charleston in Fife. He designed a huge construction which, if built, would have been three miles long and 150 feet high, and although of course it never was built, some experimental work was done in preparation for it. In 1864 a huge iron cylinder was fabricated in Burntisland, taken out to the site of the proposed bridge, and sunk into the river bed. Once in position it was weighted down with large quantities of iron and measurements taken to see how far it sank. Curiously, Bouch himself was not present to observe the experiment, which in any case was eventually abandoned, and the cylinder sold for scrap.[47]

Developments with respect to the Tay Bridge, however, were more promising, and this was due in large part to local interest in the bridge project, at least among a small group of active and influential members of the business community in Dundee. In October 1863 a meeting to discuss the bridge project was held in the offices of prominent Dundee solicitors Pattullo and Thornton, and although nothing came out of that meeting directly, the *Dundee Advertiser* was quick to register its support of the scheme. A year later, Thomas Thornton, who was to take a leading part in the promotion of the bridge project, arranged for Bouch to explain his proposals to a public meeting in the Town Council Chambers, at which he unveiled plans for a bridge between Newport and Craig Pier (the site today of Discovery Point). There were to be 63 spans, and at its highest point the bridge would tower 100 feet above high water. On the Dundee shore, the rails would curve round to the west rather than the east, and join up to the line to Perth at Magdalen Green. The audience on this occasion was largely made up of businessmen and textile industrialists, who could readily grasp the advantages of having direct and speedy access to the coalfields of Fife to fuel the steam engines driving the machinery in their mills. If there were doubters among them, daunted by the sheer scale of the project, Bouch was ready to reassure them. 'It is a very ordinary Undertaking,' he is reported to have said, 'and we have several far more stupendous and greater bridges already constructed.' Encouraged by Bouch's confidence, the great advantages of a direct rail link with Fife, and the prospect of good returns on the investment, the meeting resolved 'that it would be for the public advantage, and tend greatly to the traffic of the North of Scotland and specially the town and trade of Dundee, were the present inconvenient and expensive route to the south improved by the construction of a bridge over the River Tay.' A committee was appointed to promote the scheme, and on 4 November 1864 the prospectus of the projected Tay Bridge and Union Railway was issued, based on the capitalisation of £350,000, divided into 14,000 shares of £25 each. By mid-November plans were sufficiently far advanced that notice was given of a Parliamentary Bill to provide for the incorporation of the company, and for the construction of the bridge and connecting lines.[48]

If the promoters of the Undertaking had expected an easy passage for their bill through Parliament, they were soon to be disillusioned. While the project might be warmly welcomed by some interests, it was as warmly opposed by others, and opposition to the bill soon began to gather momentum. Naturally enough the principal opponent of the scheme was the North British Railway's great rival, the Caledonian Railway, not to mention the smaller Scottish Central and Scottish North Eastern Railways, who had no wish to see the North British extend its lines north of the Tay. In Dundee itself a powerful negative voice was that of the Harbour Board, largely composed of members of the Town Council, and jealous of the interest of the port as the principal gateway into the city for the passage of goods. Twenty miles upriver lay the city of Perth, ancient rival of Dundee, and anxious that its already diminished role as a port should not be destroyed altogether by the barrier of a bridge across its path to the open sea. In actual fact, the failure to dredge the river adequately upstream from Newburgh meant that Perth was already inaccessible to ships with masts as high as 100 feet.[49] In the end Perth Town Council was simply bought off, being promised the sum of £500 as soon as work started, plus an annual payment of £25 for every foot under the original 100 feet of clearance below the high girders. The distance was eventually set at 88 feet.[50]

This arrangement was, however, well into the future. In the meantime, in an attempt to meet some of these objections, significant changes were introduced into the plans, and these were explained in great detail to the readers of the *Advertiser* in December 1864. The site of the bridge was now to be one mile west of Newport Pier, and as it would now cross the river at a wider point than before it would be longer and include more spans – 80 instead of 63. The longest of these, over the deep water channel, was to stretch the enormous distance of 300 feet, at a height of 100 feet above the high water mark of the spring tides.[51] This was only one of many different versions of the bridge plan to be made, but it was never put to the test. Lobbying against the bridge bill by the Caledonian began to tell, support for the Undertaking began to crumble, and the promotors decided on a tactical withdrawal. The bill fell through.

In 1866 a second bill was promoted. The new scheme was significantly different from the original plan in a number of ways. On the south side, the line was to be connected not only with Tayport, but also with Leuchars, and the bridge was to cross the Tay from Wormit Bay to a point west of the Binns of Blackness. From there the rails were to be carried over the Dundee to Perth line, and then eastwards towards the centre of town by way of the gardens of the houses of Magdalen Yard Road, the Perth Road and the Nethergate, until they arrived at a magnificent new Central Station in the middle of the city.[52]

In connection with this scheme, the North British also became involved with the Town Council in a plan to develop the area to the south of the Caledonian railway line as it entered Dundee. In its 1866 bill, the railway conceded the rights of town to this area, and after the Council had successfully promoted a bill to construct the esplanade along the foreshore, the North British and the Caledonian put up £13,000 for making up the ground inland of the esplanade for railway purposes. A similar sum was contributed by the Harbour Trust towards the cost of the esplanade itself.[53]

This agreement seems to have been instrumental in overcoming the Council's opposition to the bridge proposal, and at the same time something of a truce had been reached with the Caledonian, both companies being unwilling to waste still more money on expensive legal battles. For its part, the North British withdrew its bid for the Scottish North Eastern, which both companies had had an interest in acquiring, and in return the Caledonian withdrew its opposition to the bridge, and even agreed to allow the North British use of its lines from Dundee to Aberdeen once the bridge was completed. No further obstacle now seemed to stand in the way of the project, but unfortunately at this crucial moment the North British was crippled by a severe financial crisis, brought on by overspending and weak financial management. Chairman Richard Hodgson, the great champion within the company of the bridge project, was forced out, and the second bill was withdrawn.[54]

JOHN STIRLING OF KIPPENDAVIE

The new chairman of the North British Railway Company was John Stirling of Kippendavie, a landowner and successful businessman, with many years' experience of the railway business in Scotland. Until its recent takeover by the Caledonian, he had been chairman of the Scottish North Eastern Railway. Far-sighted enough to grasp the importance of the bridge for the Company and for the east of Scotland, Stirling roused his fellow directors on the North British board in support of the bridge, and the fight was on once more. A new and less ambitious bridge scheme was adopted, involving a crossing from Wormit to Buckingham Point, curving round to the east along the line of the foreshore into a new station which was to be built on the made-up land to the north of the esplanade. From there the rails would be carried by way of a tunnel under Dock Street to join up with the line to Arbroath.

On 5 September 1869 a deputation from the North British, consisting of Stirling, Bouch and James Cox, met with members of the Town Council and the Harbour Trust. Stirling played his cards well, appealing both to the civic pride and the financial self-interest of his audience. The proposed bridge, he assured them, would be of great benefit to the coal trade of Fife, and the trade and shipping of Dundee. It would place the city directly on the main route to the north, instead of being relegated, as now, to a mere siding. With the bridge to link Dundee with the southern shore of the Tay, the journey to Edinburgh would take only an hour and a half, and only half an hour to St Andrews. The total cost, including bridge, approaches, and a tunnel to take the line eastwards under Dock Street, would not exceed £350,000, and it was the intention of the directors to guarantee a return of 5¼% to stockholders. This return, as the directors were to explain to an extraordinary meeting of the North British shareholders in November, would easily be met from the savings which would arise from doing away with the ferry across the river, and from no longer having to pay £9,000 a year to the Caledonian for the use of the Broughty Ferry to Dundee rail link. In a scheme such as this there could be no losers.

In November a public meeting was called in Dundee to promote the Tay Bridge Undertaking, a meeting which 'largely represented both the solid judgment and the youthful vigour which have enabled Dundee to take its present position as one of the most enterprising commercial towns in the kingdom.' Once again John Stirling was at his most persuasive, explaining to the assembled businessmen that of all the advantages which the bridge would bring, 'The greatest advantage of all, undoubtedly, will be the shortening of the distance between the pit mouths of Fife, and the furnaces and ship's hatchways in Dundee.' Mr Stirling, we are told, 'put this most moderately, but all businessmen instinctively appreciate it.' They no doubt also appreciated being told by Stirling that if it should happen that the bridge cost more than the estimated £350,000, then the same guarantee of 5¼% return would extend to the additional capital required to complete the project.[55] The Undertaking was launched, the subscription list was opened, and the first name on it was James Cox, chairman of the Undertaking and a director of the North British, who put himself down for 200 shares. On 15 July, 1870, the Parliamentary Bill for the Tay Bridge received the Royal Assent.[56]

THE SEER OF GOURDIE

Not everyone shared the general enthusiasm for the bridge. Prominent amongst its opponents as Parliament moved closer towards approving the scheme was farmer Patrick Matthew – the 'Seer of Gourdie' – who uttered Cassandra-like prophecies of doom in a series of eight letters to the *Advertiser* between December 1869 and March 1870. In these letters Matthew foresaw all sorts of mishaps which might befall the bridge – scouring of the foundations by the rapid flow of the river beneath; collapse of bridge supports through collision with a ship; loss of the train by centrifugal force as it took the sharp curve at the north end of the bridge; destruction of the bridge by tremors of an earthquake.[57]

The *Advertiser*, committed to the scheme, was quick to dismiss Matthew's fancies.[58] But despite his own description of himself as a 'crotchety old man with a head stuffed with old world notions, quite obsolete in the present age of progress', Matthew was very far from being a mere crank. His advice that the bridge ought to be strengthened at the north end where it curved sharply east towards Dundee preceded an announcement that just such additional piers and columns as he had suggested would be provided, and his arguments in favour of an alternative and much cheaper bridge at Newburgh were never publicly answered. Matthew's vision was of a city where the money saved by not building the Wormit bridge would be used to clean up the slums and build healthy good-quality housing for the working class, and his views on town planning were at least half a century in advance of their time. To the readers of the *Dundee Advertiser* he declared roundly, that 'I would only put the rainbow bridge, with its disposition to destruction, into the one scale, and the sanitary improvement of the impure heart of the city, alongside the superior bridge at Newburgh in the other scale; which', he asked, 'would kick the beam?'

Matthew had been particularly concerned that the bridge might be brought down perhaps by an earth tremor – the 'sleeping giant . . . whose strugglings are felt every season'. This, he thought, would be 'quite sufficient to capsize the Wormit bridge which, being so high and heavy – so crank, like a narrow boat with tall people standing in it – would be easily upset.' Few people took any notice. But before he died in September 1870, Matthew issued one final macabre warning. 'In the case of accident with a heavy passenger train,' he prophesied with fearful accuracy, 'the whole of the passengers will be killed. The eels will come to gloat over in delight the horrible wreck and banquet.'[59]

CHAPTER 3

THE BRIDGE TAKES SHAPE

⟨⟩

THE DESIGN OF THE BRIDGE

Before any bridge can be designed, especially one which is to be built across a stretch of water, the designer needs to know with certainty the nature of the ground upon which the supports of the bridge are to be built. Bouch was perfectly well aware of this, and in 1869 had commissioned 'a thoroughly experienced borer' called Jesse Wylie to survey the bed of the Tay along the line of the proposed bridge. Wylie had already surveyed the bed of the Forth for Bouch, and his report on the Tay was encouraging – with the exception only of some 250 yards on the northern side, the river was solid rock all the way across, below a layer of sand some 15 to 20 feet thick. In fact it was not – much of what Wylie had taken to be rock was no more than a layer of gravel or conglomerate, several feet thick, under which lay soft mud.[60]

Basing his design on Wylie's findings, Bouch planned a bridge which was to be 3,450 yards long – only a fraction under two miles. It would run almost due northward from Wormit across the estuary until, just before it reached the north shore, it would curve to the east, to march alongside the river and into the projected Taybridge Station. It was to consist of 89 (later reduced to 85) spans of widely different lengths – ranging from 27 feet to 200 feet (later increased to 245 feet). All but one of these (a bow-string girder near to the Dundee side) were of his favourite lattice design, as incorporated in the Belah, Deepdale and Hownes Gill Viaducts. From its beginning on the south side the bridge was to rise on a gentle gradient [1:365] to the central section, and then fall away rather more steeply [1:74] at the northward end. To maximise the height above the navigable channel for shipping to pass beneath, the 'High Girders' were placed so that their bottom rail was a continuation of the top rail of the low girders, and at this section the train would pass through rather than on top of them. The spans were to be supported on brick piers, except for the curve at the northern end, which was always intended to be built on cast-iron columns braced together with cross-ties of malleable iron.

The foundations for these columns were to be provided by pairs of iron cylinders sunk on to the river bed, lined with brick, and filled with cement.[61] As it turned out, a good many modifications to this original design had to be made in the course of construction, some of them, as we shall see, of major significance, and with a direct bearing on the bridge's collapse.

The 'Single Track' Controversy

For reasons of cost, the bridge was to carry only a single track – a decision which came in for much criticism from the local press, partly on grounds of stability, and partly on grounds of utility. The *Advertiser*, which only a few months before had been urging its readers to invest generously in the Undertaking, was now loud in its condemnation of the single track:

> In advocating a bridge across the Tay, it never occurred to us that any engineer would think of running such a spider's thread over the river as this is to be. If Mr Bouch thinks that the comparison does injustice to his plan, then we will concede that the Bridge will in the distance have the appearance of a clothes line stretched over a long row of clothes props. Approaching it somewhat nearer the clothes props will acquire the proportions of mill chimneys, and the clothes line extends to those of Blondin's tightrope. If anyone supposes that the Bridge as now planned will be a magnificent and imposing object – an addition and improvement to the noble scene of the river – he is very much deluded. Architecturally it is excessively bald and commonplace. Seeing, however, that it is proposed as a work of utility, we could excuse it not being ornamental, if there were a prospect of its being useful. But what will be the sense of attempting to carry the great East Coast route for more than two miles, suspended between the sky and the water on about the width of a respectable dining table? It assumes immense faith in railway passengers to imagine that they will trust themselves to this tightrope carried, on the south side of the river, at so great an elevation above the stream? Railway travelling will certainly

Rare engraving of the Tay Bridge as it was originally designed to be built – with brick columns instead of cast iron. *Private collection*

be made a gymnastic feat so far as this bridge is concerned, and those who love something sensational in the way of adventure need only book themselves from Wormit to Dundee.[62]

Of course it was now far too late to influence the plans, but almost a year after work on the bridge had begun the *Railway News* was still campaigning for a double track line. 'The width needed for a double line,' it pointed out 'would strengthen the architectural security of the Undertaking,' a consideration having 'special force with reference to a bridge spanning a river which is tidal, liable to enormous floods, and open to blasts of wind from the two directions that are the least merciless [sic] in their fury.'[63]

THE CONTRACTORS

Once he had received Bouch's plans and estimates, John Stirling wasted no time, and without even waiting for the agreement of his shareholders or the passage of the bill through Parliament, put the contract out to tender. There were not many takers, and of the seven tenders received, four were above Bouch's estimate. In fact the huge Undertaking was beyond the powers of all but a few, and then, even when a suitable

contractor was found – the firm of Butler and Pitts – the sudden death of Pitts before work even started forced the company to withdraw, and a substitute had to be found.

The second firm to which the work was entrusted was Charles de Bergue and Co., a highly reputable engineering firm, which undertook to complete the work within three years of the contract date of May 1871, at a cost of £217,099 18s. 6d. Under de Bergue's manager on site, Albert Grothe, and with a workforce initially of seventy men, the business of building the longest bridge in the world was begun. On a windy Saturday in July 1871, the 22nd, a small ceremony was held on the promontory above Wormit at which the foundation stone for the great bridge was laid by William Paterson, the young son of Bouch's resident engineer.[64]

But de Bergue's too ran into difficulties. Charles de Bergue was already ill at the time when the contract was signed, and he died in the spring of 1873. After his death, when the firm came under the control of his widow and daughter, it was found to be in serious financial difficulties – most of which had arisen directly from the demands of the Tay Bridge contract. In order to make sure of securing the work, Charles de Bergue had submitted a dangerously low bid, and in his estimates he had made no proper allowance for any increase in costs along the way. His company was owed money for work already carried out on the bridge, while its own creditors were pressing hard for re-payment.

Bouch himself took a hand it trying to retrieve the situation. He urged the North British directors to pay for work done, but at the same time expressed concern that the firm was now controlled by two women, and as he wrote later, 'Finding that the works could not well go on under them, it was deemed advisable to get the representatives of de Bergue to renounce and give up the contract.' Given that the firm's difficulties had arisen from the decisions of Charles de Bergue, and not the two women, this may seem more than a little unfair, but the outcome was that de Bergue's withdrew, leaving the whole enterprise in disarray. The situation was discussed between Bouch and Grothe in detail at a meeting in London, following which Grothe wrote a long letter outlining one possible solution to the problem, that is that the Company should dispense with a regular contractor altogether, and instead employ Grothe himself as overall manager of the project, in return for an annual salary of £1,000. Penalty clauses in the proposed agreement would ensure that the deadline for completion would be met, and further delay in finding a replacement for de Bergue's would be avoided. The directors, however, rejected this proposal in favour of finding new contractors.

It took a further three months to engage a successor – Hopkins Gilkes & Co. of Middlesbrough – whose senior partner, Edgar Gilkes, had worked with Bouch on the construction of the Belah Viaduct, which they had completed in record time. One of the first decisions of the new contractors was to confirm Albert Grothe as their resident manager, and the work continued without any further delay.[65]

BUILDING THE BRIDGE

How does one build a bridge of this magnitude? Up until that time, the orthodox method of building a bridge across water was to construct staging along the line of the bridge, fabricate the girders on the staging, and then transfer them on to the supports built alongside. Given the weather conditions along the Tay, in particular the combination of sudden high winds and fierce tidal currents, this was not a feasible plan, and new methods had to be devised. At this stage, de Bergue's were still the contractors, and they decided to make the parts for the bridge

One of the pontoons used to carry the bridge supports. *Dundee City Library*

at their workshops in Cardiff and Manchester, and transport them to
an on-site fabrication yard which they set up on the shores of Wormit
Bay. Here too they built a complex of offices, workshops, and facilities
for their workmen, which included at Grothe's insistence dormitories,
a dining hall, and even a reading room.[66] Down at the river's edge they
built a wharf standing 80 yards out into the Tay, and wooden staging
on which the girders would first be assembled, and then floated out on
huge barges to where they would be raised up onto their columns of
brick by means of hydraulic jacks.

Before this could be done, however, the bridge supports had to be
constructed. To begin with the original plan was adhered to, that is to
make each of the piers out of two cylinders of wrought iron, eight and
a half feet in diameter. Once each of pair of cylinders had been made
on the shore, they were attached to two pontoons, one on each side,
taken out to their assigned position, and lowered on to the river bed.
The *Advertiser* explained the procedure to its readers in some detail in
October 1871:

> The cylinders . . . are prepared in three parts joined together
> – a malleable iron cylindrical base, a sur-base shaped like a
> truncated cone, also of malleable iron, and overall the cylinder
> itself, made of cast iron. The top of the sur-base is closed over
> with a plate of the same strength as the outer skin, a hole being
> left in the centre to enable the divers to clear out and build

The Bridge under construction. *Dundee City Library*

A completed girder on the jetty. *Dundee City Library*

in the under portion of the pillar. Upon the platform thus formed, the interior of the cylinder is built up of solid brick and cement, having also the centre space free. To float these masses of material, two pontoons have been constructed by Mr Austin, bearing four strong malleable iron girders. On each girder is placed a hydraulic ram capable of raising 60 tons, and the pontoon being floated so as to bring the centre between the girders, the mass is floated off, and sunk by means of the rams into its proper site.[67]

Once they were in place, the tops of the cylinders were sealed, an air-bell was attached, and all the water inside the columns was pumped out. It was then the task of the workmen to climb down into the cylinders and dig out the mud, gravel and sand on the river bed until the cylinder had sunk down on to the firm rock underneath. The next stage was to build a thick lining of brick inside the cylinder, and finally fill the core of the construction with cement. The first nine piers from the Wormit end were made in this way, and then a method was devised of making them as one complete construction on a large base, so that up to twelve men could work inside at one time, thus speeding up the time

A caisson with workmen. *Dundee City Library*

Inside a caisson, showing workmen excavating the river bed with hand tools.
Victor Bignell

needed to install them. Once the piers were completed the girders were floated out on pontoons and positioned on the piers, then gradually lifted up as the columns were built up under them.[68]

Such a description gives no idea of the rigours of the work. Men laboured within the narrow cylinders, or *caissons*, in shifts of twelve hours at a time in candlelight, day and night, in bitter cold and stifling heat, and always with the threat of disaster, for if a cylinder settled awkwardly on to the river bottom they could be trapped beneath it, or drowned as the water rushed in and overwhelmed them. (Later the invention by the engineer Frank Beattie of a steam-driven pump to excavate the silt led to significant savings in time and improvements in safety.) For those working high up on the bridge girders there was the danger of being swept off into the sea by a sudden gust. As the *Advertiser* had warned when the first work began:

> One of the chief difficulties the contractors will have to contend against will doubtless be the heavy gales of wind from the west. Mr Patrick Matthew has predicted the danger of the

A steam-driven vacuum pump used to excavate silt.
Dundee City Library

41

Bridge being destroyed by some of these gales. There is no reason why they should blow over the Tay Bridge any more than many other great bridges, but it is not improbable that they may once and again do considerable damage while the work is in progress.[69]

No-one was more sensitive to public anxiety about the safety of the bridge than the contractor's chief engineer, Albert Grothe. A popular figure in Dundee, and much in demand as a lecturer on the construction of the bridge, Grothe took every opportunity to reassure his audiences. To those who questioned the security of the piers, he answered confidently that 'the foundations of the piers would all be on rock'. The piers themselves would be enormously heavy – the smaller 9 foot 6 inch ones weighing some 700 tons, and the large 13 foot 6 inch ones 1,500 tons. He then did a calculation to show that the maximum pressure which would be exerted on the concrete of the piers by the weight of the superstructure – pillars, girders, and the train itself – could never exceed 6 tons per square foot, while concrete of the quality to be used could withstand a pressure of 80 tons.

To those who worried about the effect of a large vessel colliding with the bridge supports he was equally reassuring, and his statement throws some interesting light on the state of bridge engineering of the day. 'The superstructure,' he conceded, 'looked very light, but it only looked so. Engineers were well up in these matters now. It was twenty-seven years since wrought iron was used for bridge building, and it was a hundred since iron bridges were built in England. The duty of the engineer was not now a question of calculating merely the strength of the girder, but it was the understanding and selection of that system which gave most strength with the least waste of material.' Moreover great care was taken to make sure that the iron used for the bridge was of the highest quality. Samples were regularly sent for testing to the establishment of Mr David Kirkaldy in London, and 'every bit of iron which had a square section of one inch had to stand a tensile strain of 22 tons, or it would never have the honour of forming part of the Tay Bridge. (Cheers.)'

In view of the ultimate fate of the bridge, one of the key questions which Grothe had to address was that of the ability of the bridge to resist the pressure of the wind. 'Supposing,' he put to his audience, 'that there were a heavy westerly gale and a train was going over the bridge, what would be the effect?' According to his calculations:

Grothe's signature on a window-pane of the house where he stayed while the Bridge was being constructed. *Ann Bridges/Roland Paxton*

It would require a westerly gale of 90 tons pressure at the top of the pier on the square foot to knock the pier over standing on the bare rock . . . Now with what pressure did the wind blow? The pressure which the gale would have had at the top of the pier which wrecked the *Royal George* was 21 tons, while he had shown that not less a pressure than 90 tons was necessary to blow the pier over. (Great applause.) But some people might say, supposing a cyclone or a typhoon which visits India were to come here. What would the consequence be? The total pressure of the severest typhoon that has ever happened would be equal to 42 tons against the pier, but then it would require 90 tons before the pier could be upset. (Great applause.) Now where were they to get a wind strong enough to do that?[70]

A Catalogue of Accidents

There were in fact a number of accidents which occurred during the construction of the bridge, some of them fatal. Two men were drowned when three cylinders on the south bank collapsed and pinned them down in the mud. When number 14 pier was being filled with cement, a vent which should have allowed the air to escape became clogged and the air pressure built up until it blew out a plate. This in turn caused an air-bell and its engine to fall onto a barge below and kill two men. The worst incident, in which six men died, took place in the early hours of Tuesday 26 August 1873. The accident happened in one of the caissons which had been floated out and sunk into position, and inside which the night shift of a foreman and seven men were digging out the gravel and mud. An air-bell was being used to pressurise the caisson to help keep the water out, the normal pressure being between 12 and 20 lbs per square inch. One man and a sixteen-year-old boy were up above the air-bell, in charge of the engine for the air pump. No-one knows exactly what went wrong, but at 2.30 a.m., just as foreman Johnston had come out of the air lock for a breath of fresh air, he felt a sudden rush of wind past him, and heard the screech of metal against metal. The explosion flung the boy, William White, into the river, where by great good fortune he was able to swim to a small boat tied to one of the barges. Paddling the boat with his hands, he was able to pick up the other engineman, Anderson, who was no swimmer and was on the point of drowning. They were also able to rescue the foreman and one other workman, Farquar, but the rest were dead, either killed by the explosion, or drowned by the inrush of water into the cylinder.

There was no public inquiry, as there would have been today, but Grothe carried out one of his own without much success. The pressure gauge showed a pressure of only 14 lbs – well within the normal range for safe working. Grothe's opinion, which Bouch relayed to the directors of the North British, was that a coal barge moored nearby had swung against the caisson and broken a plate, leading to an explosion as the air rushed out, but there was no evidence to support this theory. The only good to come out of this incident was that Grothe ruled that in future no shift would last longer than eight hours, and that to compensate the men for the loss of earnings he would raise the rate of pay from eight to ten pence an hour. Altogether the bridge cost the lives of twenty workmen, together of course with the passengers and crew lost in its collapse.[71]

Not all the accidents which befell the bridge were caused by human misjudgements or the failure of machinery. The weather was often to blame both for loss of life, as men were swept off the bridge by sudden gusts of wind, and for various setbacks to the progress of construction. As Albert Grothe himself commented after the bridge was finally completed, 'The most notable difficulties in connection

with the construction of the Tay Bridge were caused by the boister-
ous character of the weather on the river.' In 1872 a gale blew for
three weeks without a pause, making work on the water impossible,
and in 1874 an unusually hard winter saw ice floes on the Tay which
likewise stopped work for weeks on end. In August 1876 one of the
high girders was being towed out to the bridge on its pontoons when
one of the tugs broke down. A strong wind was blowing at the time,
and the one remaining tug was powerless to prevent the girder being
swept downriver towards Broughty Ferry. Just in time a second tug
came out from Dundee to the rescue, and the girder was recovered
and positioned safely on its cutwaters by late evening. A more serious
and expensive incident occurred in February 1877, again as the result
of gale-force winds, coincidentally involving the same span which had
broken away the previous August. On this later occasion, on 2 February, the girder and its neighbour had been successfully floated out to
their positions on the bridge, where they were to form the spans joining
piers 28 and 29, and 29 and 30. By mid-afternoon they had been raised
by hydraulic rams to a height just above their final position on the tops
of the columns, and were being supported by temporary lifting battens
while the work of constructing the tops of the columns upon which
they would finally rest was being completed. At four o'clock a sudden
fierce gale struck the bridge, sending the workmen scurrying for cover,
and then at 8 p.m. a particularly furious gust blew the two unsecured
girders down from their perches, taking with them both their own supporting columns, and the next girder along. Falling from a height of
some 90 feet above the water level, they crashed down on the wreckage
of the columns which had preceded them, becoming severely damaged
in the process. One was in too bad a state to be salvaged, and for the
time being was left where it fell, but the other was retrieved, sent back
to Middlesbrough to be straightened out, and replaced on the span of
the high girders nearest to the Wormit end of the bridge. The cost of
this accident was estimated at some £3,000.[72]

A RADICAL REDESIGN

In some ways the worst accident to befall the bridge, before its final
tragic collapse, had taken place even before the plans for its design had
been prepared. As we have seen, Wylie's report that the river bed was
solid rock for almost the entire distance across the estuary had been the

basis upon which Bouch had drawn up his designs. When it was discovered in 1873, not long after the death of Charles de Bergue, that the report was inaccurate, the discovery inevitably forced radical changes in those designs, changes which were to affect the construction and arguably the integrity of the whole structure.

The basic problem was that, after the fourteenth pier from the south side had been placed in position on the river bed, what had been reported to be solid rock was found to be no more than a thin layer of conglomerate – compacted boulders and gravel – covering a great depth of mud, and of course with much less strength to support the enormous weight of the bridge. At the north end also, problems with mud had seriously delayed progress with the curved section, and when an attempt was made in late 1872 to erect the brick columns for the straight section at this end, the foundations kept giving way. Bouch seems to have taken this serious blow entirely in his stride, and informed the directors that 'there is no difficulty whatever in making good foundations on this material.' Grothe likewise was apparently unconcerned by the news about the borings, which, he explained blandly to an audience in March 1876, 'had turned out to be rather different from what they had been expected to be.' 'The gravel', he assured his listeners, 'was perfectly safe as a foundation, but it was not as solid as rock.'[73]

It was thought that all that was required to make a sound foundation on gravel was to increase the area of its base, in order to reduce the pressure exerted by the weight of the bridge superstructure on the foundations from the 6½ tons per square foot originally planned, to 4½. This, it was said, could easily be accomplished by sinking huge iron caissons filled with cement on which the piers would rest. Unfortunately it was not so simple. Bouch got his assistant Allan D. Stewart to check his calculations – Stewart was the mathematician in Bouch's team – and his conclusion was that the pressure would have to be reduced still further – to 2¾ tons. To achieve this would require not just the enlargement of the piers, but a major redesign of the columns resting on those piers – the columns which in turn held up the girders and track on which the trains would run. Bouch's solution, perhaps not surprisingly, was to replace the columns of brick with columns consisting of cast-iron tubes braced together with malleable iron cross-ties – a system which he had used so often and so successfully on his previous railway viaducts over land. The intention initially was to construct these

Bouch up on the high girders. *Dundee City Library*

new piers from iron columns in groups of eight, but when it was found that even the new large caissons were not wide enough to take eight columns, Bouch reduced the number to six, arranged in an elongated hexagonal shape supported by an iron baseplate, itself resting on six-sided brickwork constructions made on shore and floated out to its caisson by pontoon. The columns themselves were quite slender, some 15 and some 18 inches in diameter, and cast in 10-foot lengths which were then joined together end to end by bolts through flanges. The columns were also cast with lugs on the sides to which cross-bracing was bolted, and where the bottoms of the columns rested on their supporting bases, they were secured by holding down bolts capable of taking a load of some 200 tons.

The new bases were to be massive affairs of concrete, 20 feet thick and over 30 feet across, topped by their hexagonal cutwaters of brick and masonry. Their sheer size and weight required the adoption of new methods of construction. While in many parts of the river bed there was a layer of rocks and gravel sufficiently strong to support the weight of the caissons, in others there was not, and arrangements were made to bring in a team of experienced pile drivers from Holland, under the management of Gerard Camphuis, to secure the foundations. To speed up the job of excavating the foundations, Frank Beattie, one of the site engineers, devised an ingenious and effective sand pump, like an enormous vacuum cleaner, which was operated by divers working on the river bed.[74]

As all this represented an unwelcome and unplanned increase in costs, to save money Bouch reduced the number of spans, and there-fore the number of bases required to support them. The high girders were reduced from fourteen 200-foot girders to thirteen, that is eleven girders of 245 feet and two of 227 feet, while three more piers were saved among the low girders. An inevitable consequence of the substi-tution of cast-iron towers for columns of masonry was that the bases were now too small to allow for the kind of inclined side supports which had been a feature of Bouch's land-based viaducts.[75]

Having made his decision, Bouch wrote to the Board to explain his thinking. In order to reduce the pressure on the bases, he had decided to build the bridge supports of 'strong iron columns', beginning the ironwork about five feet above the level of the spring tides to reduce the corrosive action of the salt water. As well as being much lighter than the original brick, he claimed that the new iron columns would have

The high girders being lifted into position onto their columns.
Dundee City Library

several extra advantages – they would be cheaper, stronger, and would be easier to erect. The only drawback he could see was that they would have to be repainted every three years at a cost of £200.[76]

THE WORMIT FOUNDRY

It does not seem to have occurred to anyone at the time to ask why, if the iron columns were such an improvement over the brick, they had not been specified in the first place, but the Board was in no position to quibble. The alternative to Bouch's iron columns was no bridge at all, and that they could not afford to contemplate. But the change of plan was by no means so economical or so simple to achieve as Bouch had led them to believe. For one thing it meant scrapping large quantities of ironwork prepared for the original design, and also, of course, it would require the casting of large numbers of new columns. At this point the management of de Bergue's (this was before the change of contractors to Gilkes and Co.) made an important decision, which in the opinion of one commentator at least, 'was to have a disastrous effect on the subsequent fate of the bridge'. They decided to cast the columns themselves at a foundry they built for the purpose at Wormit.[77]

The foundry was largely the work of Frank Beattie, a former chief draughtsman from de Bergue's, and one of the most experienced engineers working on the bridge contract. Beattie had designed the foundry as a simple rectangular one-storey building equipped with a small steam engine to drive the lathe, the multiple drilling machine and the fan for the furnace. The crucible for melting the iron was placed outside the building, with a trough leading from it to the interior to carry the molten iron to the moulds. Inside there was a travelling crane capable of lifting a load of eight tons, and moving it to any part of the building.

Both the working conditions and the standards of workmanship were to come in for a good deal of criticism during the Inquiry. Some, but by no means all, was justified. It was common practice for the cores of the moulds to be dampened with salt rather than fresh water, and whatever the alleged advantages of this practice for reducing impurities on molten metal, it inevitably produced quantities of acrid fumes. The iron supplied for casting – known as Cleveland no. 3 – was not of the best quality, and the use of low grade metal led to poor quality castings, as the molten pig iron refused to run easily into the moulds. Sometimes the metal fused with the casting sand to produce a scab on the surface of the column; at other times air bubbles left the surface pock-marked

Wormit Foundry. *Dundee City Library*

Wormit Foundry. *Dundee City Library*

with holes. Imperfections of this kind were disguised by filling them
with a substance known as 'beaumont egg', a mixture of wax, iron
filings and lamp black, which when rubbed over with a stone looked
just like the cast metal. Some of the columns came out of their moulds
with imperfectly cast lugs, and these had to be made good by a process
known as 'burning on'. Few experienced moulders would deny that
burned-on lugs were weaker than properly cast ones, but on the other
hand there is very little firm evidence to show that that any columns
with burned-on lugs were actually incorporated into the structure of
the bridge. What certainly is true is that the holes in the lugs were
universally cast rather than drilled, with the result that the holes come
out conical in shape rather than cylindrical. It was to be claimed at the
Inquiry that these conical holes were partly to blame for weaknesses in
the cross-bracing of the columns.[78]

Problems with the contractors and with the river bed, the need to
redesign the bridge, and the delays caused by the weather and various
accidents all help to explain the slow progress made in building the
bridge, and the growing impatience of the North British directors. In
July 1876 Stirling offered Edgar Gilkes a bonus of £2,000 if a train could
be passed over the bridge on 1 September of the following year, raising

51

the bonus soon after by a further £500. But in February 1877 the two high girders blew off their piers, and Gilkes insisted that the September deadline could be met only if two new spans were constructed, rather than repairing and re-using one of the damaged ones. Reluctant to authorise the additional expense of two new girders, Stirling agreed to extend the deadline by two more weeks, and increased the value of the bonus to 4,000 guineas, on the condition that on the appointed day a train of forty coal wagons, with two engines and two brake-vans should cross the bridge. After some private misgivings, Gilkes wrote back to George Wieland, the North British secretary, assuring him that the bridge would be finished by 15 September, 'trusting to your usual consideration should we be a day or two short in our calculations'.[79] In the event, the first train to cross the bridge did so on 26 September 1877, only eleven days over the deadline.

SOME EMINENT VISITORS

Not surprisingly, the building of the bridge was an object of great interest to the people of the area, and to visitors from many parts of the world. Some were professional engineers, anxious to learn or perhaps to criticise; some were newsmen, with a brief to bring their papers' readers up to date with the progress of the bridge; while others were celebrities, whose visits were newsworthy occasions in themselves.

One visitor, in the early days of 1876, was the correspondent of *The Times*, whose 'first impression, received from a glance at the works, is the extreme tenuity of the line the bridge will ultimately present. It is constructed for a single line of rails, and its fine outline seems but ill adapted to stand the stormy seas and furious gales for which the river is famous.' A closer inspection was found to be more reassuring – 'the structure presenting, on careful examination, the idea of great strength and solidity.' The observer made his way to the high ground at the south end of the bridge, where he discovered Albert Grothe's office, as well as the various 'store rooms, refreshment rooms, lodgings for such of the men as reside permanently at the works, and other buildings.'

'Here also', he noted,

> has been erected an iron foundry, where the innumerable cast
> iron pillars etc. to be used in the structure have been cast,

planed, drilled, and prepared for use. Below, on the water's edge, are extensive stores of bricks, cement, and other materials, while two jetties present a scene of much activity as groups of workmen build up and rivet together the lattice girders which are to span the piers . . . Between the jetties singular structures of brick and iron are being put together, while the fleet of floating pontoons, barges, tugs and steam launches show the apparatus by which the huge masses are carried out into the river, and by which the work of sinking and fixing them is carried on and superintended.[80]

Amongst the celebrities who came to pay homage to the bridge were the Emperor of Brazil, in July 1877, and Prince Leopold of the Belgians, who arrived at Newport in September 1877, crossed the river on the ferry accompanied by Thomas Bouch, and was taken out to the high girders on a wagon drawn by a ballast engine. Earlier that same month the bridge had received an even more distinguished visitor in the person of the former President of the United States, Ulysses S. Grant, perhaps better known in Britain as the general who won the American Civil War for the North. He arrived from Edinburgh on 1 September, together with Sir James Falshaw, the Lord Provost of Edinburgh, Mr and Mrs Bouch, and a large entourage of hangers-on. They were met at Tayport by James Cox and Edgar Gilkes, then escorted to the harbour where the tug *Excelsior* was to carry them over the river (the plaque marking the occasion may still be seen on the wall of one of the harbour buildings). En route they called on the *Mars* training ship, where they were piped aboard and given a tour round the ship. This concluded with a suitably uplifting speech from Sir James, who solemnly advised the boys to 'strive to be good men and useful members of society'. 'There may be generals among them,' suggested Cox, but this was going too far for Falshaw. 'If there may not be many generals among you, boys, there will be many corporals among you at least. (Cheers.) You will all get on by good conduct, and steady and patient perseverance.'[81]

The party carried on to Dundee and the customary lunch presided over by Cox. With lunch there were more speeches, and after lunch came the obligatory visit to the bridge itself, the party walking out on to the structure until they were about a mile from the north shore. Still more speeches, and the presentation of a book of photographs prepared by Mr Valentine, the well-known Dundee photographer, showing the bridge in its various stages of construction. Grant's laconic comment on these wonders – probably apocryphal – 'It's a very long bridge.'[82]

CHAPTER 4

THE TAY IS BRIDGED

⟫⦁⟪

FINISHED AT LAST

And so at long last the bridge was finished. It had taken six hundred men six years to build, using 10,000,000 bricks and 2,000,000 rivets, 87,000 cubic feet of timber, 15,000 casks of cement, 3,700 tons of cast iron and 3,500 tons of malleable iron. It had cost the lives of twenty workmen, and over £300,000. Let William McGonagall mark the occasion in his inimitable fashion:

> Beautiful Railway Bridge of the Silvery Tay!
> I hope that God will protect all passengers
> By night and by day,
> And that no accident will befall them while crossing
> The Bridge of the Silvery Tay,
> For that would be most awful to be seen,
> Near by Dundee and the Magdalen Green[83]

The correspondent of *The Times* was less lyrical, but he also sought to reassure himself that the structure was stronger and safer than it looked:

> It was so long and so loft, and yet so narrow that when seen from the heights above Newport it looks like a mere cable slung from shore to shore; and seeing a train puffing along it for the first time excited the same kind of nervousness as must have been felt by those who watched Blondin crossing Niagara. Fragile as its appearance is, however, there is no doubt about its thorough stability.[84]

THE FIRST TRAIN

The first train to cross, if one discounts the work engines trundling along the rails with materials for the bridge builders, was the *Lochee,*

The Directors' Special makes the first crossing by a passenger train on 26 September, 1877. *Dundee City Library*

which on 26 September 1877 carried a full complement of the directors of the North British Railway Company and their guests.

Prior to that, Bouch had taken care that the ironwork of the bridge should be thoroughly prepared, a process which included the tightening of the gib and cotter tensioning device in each bracing bar before any trains went over the bridge. At one point Albert Grothe was approached by the contractor who was engaged in excavating the tunnel beside the harbour wall for permission to run trains over the bridge carrying excavated material to the south side of the river. When consulted by Grothe, Bouch made the position abundantly clear:

> I dare not risk any engine on the bridge until the ties are properly tightened and bear their share of the strain. If any idea were entertained of running an engine on the bridge before this is done, I would immediately resign the engineership to escape responsibility and, moreover, I would consider it my duty to report the matter to the Procurator Fiscal.[85]

By 26 September, this work had been duly carried out. It was a fine day, and the engine shone in its green livery and gleaming brass, pulling behind it a saloon, a first-class coach, and two brake vans. John Stirling was there, and John Beaumont, the deputy chairman, Sir James Falshaw and a number of Scottish MPs. Starting from Burntisland, the train stopped at Leuchars to pick up the local dignitaries from Dundee, including the chairman of the Tay Bridge Undertaking, James Cox, and the MP for Dundee, James Yeaman. The engine itself was driven not by a regular engine driver, but by Dugald Drummond, the legendary locomotive superintendent for the Company. Setting off again from Leuchars, Drummond brought the train to a halt at the southern end of the bridge to pick up some more important passengers, including Mrs Bouch, while her husband had the fun of riding on the footplate of the pilot engine which ran before them across the bridge.

'The scene presented,' enthused the *Advertiser*, which had forgotten its earlier opposition to a single line bridge,

> was one not likely to be speedily effaced from the recollection of those by whom it was witnessed. High up in the air was the train moving majestically along what, viewed from distant shores, seems a thread-like support. Below were the steamers dancing about on the silver waters, their occupants jubilant with delight that they had been privileged to witness the consummation of one of the most remarkable triumphs of

Looking along the high girders from the inside.
St Andrews University, Valentine Collection

engineering skill; and the crowds on the Dundee side lining
the Esplanade and covering Magdalen Green cheering and
waving their hats and handkerchiefs enthusiastically.

The journey across the bridge took exactly fifteen minutes, or about
three times as long as it would take the regular passenger service once
the bridge came into full operation. As the train crossed the high girders,
the roof-lights on one of the carriages collided with some wooden scaffolding, and were carried away into the swirling waters below. 'Some
of the more timorous passengers were thrown into a slight momentary
alarm', but they were quickly reassured, and the cavalcade soon arrived
safely in the marshalling yards (Taybridge Station itself was yet to be
completed) and the dignitaries alighted for the ceremonial lunch. Once
that was over they re-entered the train and disappeared back again over
the bridge in the direction of Edinburgh.[86]

It would be another eight months before the general public would
be able to share the experience of crossing the bridge by train, but
there was no doubt in the minds of Bouch's fellow engineers, or some
of them at any rate, that he had achieved a notable success. And if
the Tay Bridge were a success, then it could be only a matter of time
before Bouch's grand design of carrying the line over both Forth and
Tay was accomplished. W.H. Barlow, who was in due course to figure
as a member of the three-man inquiry into the collapse, and to be the
architect of the new replacement Tay Bridge, was, in October 1877,
unstinting in his praise for his fellow engineer. In a letter to a colleague,
he wrote of Bouch's plan:

The bridge completed at last.

I am not at all without hope that this great work will yet be carried into effect. Mr Bouch's great Tay Bridge is a success which familiarises the minds of capitalists with large engineering works capable of earning their money's worth, and as to the span of the structure, I saw a bridge of like span last year in the course of construction between New York and Brooklyn. With such examples I shall not give up hope that the crowning work of Mr Bouch will yet be accomplished.[87]

BOARD OF TRADE INSPECTION

Although the directors had had their first run over the bridge, the crossing could not be opened to the public without inspection and certification by the Board of Trade. The inspector despatched for the purpose was a former military engineer, Major General Charles Hutchinson, R.E. Hutchinson spent three days from 25 to 27 February 1878, examining and testing every, or almost every, aspect of the bridge. He ran ballast engines across it, starting with a single engine and working up to six. He ran them across the high girders, and used a theodolite to measure the amount of lateral oscillation, which he found to be 'nothing at all excessive, as far as my judgment went'. He examined the ironwork, and reported that it 'has been well put together both in the columns and the girders.' The one test he did not make – indeed could not make without a convenient storm – was to observe the bridge in a gale. He was not unaware of this omission, and at the end of his report he noted that 'When again visiting this spot, I should wish if possible to have an opportunity to observe the effects of a high wind when a train of carriages is running over the bridge.'[88] Apart from this observation he made no mention of the effect of wind pressure on the bridge, and given the prominence of this issue as a factor in the collapse of the bridge, his attitude may be significant. At the Court of Inquiry he was quite explicit: 'The subject of wind pressure never entered into the calculations that I made, and never has done . . . We have no data whatever to go upon with regard to wind pressure. It has never been, to my knowledge, customary to take wind pressure into account in calculating the parts of bridges of this description.'[89]

He had only a few suggestions for improvements – mostly trivial. There ought, he advised, to be supports across the rails at right angles to keep them the correct distance apart. At one or two places there was some slackness in the rails, and this should be seen to. In order to reduce expansion of the girders in the summer heat, he proposed they should be painted white. He also cautioned against allowing trains to pass over the bridge at excessive speeds, and suggested a speed limit of 25 miles per hour.

And so the bridge was finished, and if it differed in some respects from the original design, what did that matter now? Not only was the bridge finished, but so also were the approach rails joining the bridge to the existing rail system, north and south. So too were the new stations along the route, of which by far the grandest was Dundee's Taybridge Station, built of Bannockburn stone, and filled with all kinds of modern amenities. Its long central platform was covered from end to end by a huge glass-paned roof, beneath which might be found no fewer than three refreshment rooms and three classes of ladies waiting rooms, as well as lavatories and offices. At its eastern end lay the great tunnel leading upwards to the docks, and beyond them along the coast to Arbroath and Aberdeen.

THE OFFICIAL OPENING

But before the public could enjoy full access to these facilities, there had to be one more ceremony – the official opening of the bridge, planned for 31 May, 1878. There had been hopes that for this occasion Queen Victoria herself could be persuaded to come out of her long seclusion and perform the ceremony, but these hopes were not realised. In the event the honour fell upon James Cox, an honour to which, as chairman of the Undertaking, he had a rightful claim.

For once the weather was fine and the water calm, which was just as well as the arrangements required that the dignitaries from Dundee should first travel across the river in the ferry, *Auld Reekie*, before making their way to Leuchars station to join up with the party from Edinburgh. These gentlemen with their ladies had taken the familiar route from Waverley station to Granton, crossing the Forth on the steamer *John Stirling* to Burntisland, where the special train was waiting to take them across Fife to Leuchars. At Leuchars they were joined by the Dundee party, and soon the train, consisting of a number of first-class carriages, carrying some fifteen hundred people and drawn by the gallant *Lochee*, pulled out of the station. A few minutes later they passed through St Fort, the last station on the line before the bridge,

The Piper o' Dundee celebrates the public opening of the bridge, 31 May 1878. *Dundee City Library*

past Thomas Barclay's signal box, and then on to the bridge itself. At a steady pace, never exceeding the stipulated 25 mph, the train moved along the bridge, through the high girders, down the sloping section on the north side, round the curve on the shore line, where thousands of spectators standing on Magdalen Green waved and cheered, and into Taybridge Station. Here they were greeted by Provost Robertson, who shook John Stirling warmly by the hand and bid him welcome. Amid the cheers of the bystanders, James Cox spoke of the bridge over the Tay as 'a structure worthy of this enlightened age', which he now declared to be officially open, and the party moved off in a procession behind the band of the Forfarshire Volunteers in the direction of the Albert Institute and the banquet which awaited those fortunate enough to have received an invitation. But before the gathering could sit down for lunch, one more ceremony had to take place – the granting of the freedom of the city to both Stirling and Bouch, agreed at a meeting of the Town Council only that morning. Stirling was there to receive it, of course, but Bouch was not. Never keen on public display, he had not come to the celebrations at all, preferring to send his apologies and mention disarmingly that he was fully engaged in designing the successor to the Tay Bridge – the bridge that would span the Forth.

Later that year, however, on 9 August, at a separate ceremony, Bouch was presented with the freedom of the city by Provost Robertson. His thoughts were evidently very much on the new venture. In accepting the honour, he said that 'it was a matter of regret . . . that the Tay Bridge was built for a single line, but guided by the experience gained, the bridge across the Forth was to be made for a double line'.[90] And so it was, of course, but not by Bouch.

THE BRIDGE IN OPERATION

The passenger rail service using the new bridge began on Saturday, 1 June, 1878. The Company had already announced the new timetable – they would run seven trains a day each way between Edinburgh and Dundee, the first train from Dundee leaving at 6.25 a.m. For those travelling all the way to Edinburgh, and therefore having to catch the first ferry crossing the Forth, the best plan would be to wait for the 7.15, which connected with the ferry at Burntisland at half past eight. The combined ferry crossing and train journey into Edinburgh accounted for a further hour and five minutes, making a total travelling time of two hours and twenty minutes, or about one hour less than the old pre-bridge journey.

In the early days the journey across the bridge became a popular outing, with passengers from Dundee buying tickets for the short trip to St Fort or Leuchars (ninepence for a ticket to St Fort) and making a picnic of it, but the long-term value of the bridge to the company lay in its ability to attract passenger and goods traffic away from the Caledonian. The early morning passenger from Waverley to Dundee now had a choice between leaving at 6.15 a.m. on the Caledonian train which arrived in Dundee at 9.45, or of taking the North British train leaving at 6.40, but still getting to Dundee at two minutes past nine, almost three-quarters of an hour before its rival. Moreover, with the opening of the bridge, under previous agreements, the North British was entitled to run its trains over the Caledonian line to Aberdeen via Arbroath.

The outcome was hardly surprising. By the end of the first year of operation, it was estimated, the North British was carrying 84% of the Edinburgh-Dundee traffic, and 59% of the traffic between Edinburgh and Aberdeen. The volume of traffic between Dundee and the towns and villages of Fife had doubled. Perhaps more important than the increase in passenger business was the increase in the carriage of freight, especially coal from the Fife coal mines. In only six months, goods traffic to Dundee had risen by 40 per cent.

In terms of the railway business in Scotland, the bridge had led directly to the supremacy of the North British over its powerful rivals. It now commanded the largest rail operation in the country, carrying over 15 million passengers a year, and with a gross annual revenue of more than £2 million. The bridge had done everything John Stirling and the promoters of the Undertaking had hoped for. The value of shares in the company rose by 30 percent.[91]

THE QUEEN CROSSES THE BRIDGE

Only one final accolade was missing – the actual presence of the Queen. If the directors had not been too surprised at her refusal to attend the opening ceremony, there was no good reason in their opinion why she should not at least travel over the bridge on her way south from Balmoral, rather than take the overland route via Perth. And indeed that was already the royal intention, signalled by a test run of the royal train, empty of passengers, across the bridge and back again towards the end of June, 1879. Moreover, with a little subtle persuasion by representatives of Dundee's Town Council, Her Majesty also agreed to have her train pause briefly at Taybridge Station, for her to receive a civic address through the window of her carriage.

What an occasion! It made the previous ceremonies to honour the bridge seem quiet affairs by comparison. All along the route of the train crowds gathered to wave and cheer. In Dundee the flags were out in the streets, ships in the harbour were covered in bunting, and the boys on the *Mars* were drawn up on deck in their smartest uniforms. At the station a huge collection of important people stood waiting for the train to arrive – headed by Provost Brownlie, clutching the address of welcome which he would shortly read to the royal visitor. Sure enough, at 5.57 p.m. the train emerged from the Dock Street tunnel in a cloud of steam, and came to rest in front of the delegation to the strains of the National Anthem. The address was read, Bouch, Stirling and Cox were presented, and the brief visit was over. The train pulled away towards the bridge which it took at half the normal speed, while the boys on the *Mars* stood rigidly to attention and the ship's guns fired the salute. There was an epilogue. On 27 June 1879, Thomas Bouch was knighted at Windsor Castle, along with, amongst others, Henry Bessemer, inventor of the Bessemer iron-smelting process.[92]

Doubts Set in

And yet not everyone was happy with the bridge. A number of regular passengers on the line began to be concerned at the speed of the train as it made the crossing, which they calculated was much faster than the 25 mph stipulated by the Board of Trade. One, former Dundee Provost William Robertson, went so far as to abandon his season ticket on the railway and revert to using the ferry. Robertson also complained to the stationmaster at Taybridge, James Smith, who spoke to at least one of the drivers. John Leng, editor and owner of the *Dundee Advertiser*, was also convinced that the trains were going too fast, and he complained of a 'curious prancing motion, as the carriages passed over the bridge, quite unlike the normal behaviour of a train on solid ground'. He mentioned all this to Smith and to Henry Noble, who had been in charge of brickwork construction on the bridge, and was now the Company's Inspector for the whole structure. After the bridge came into service, the Dundee Water Commissioners laid a six-inch water pipe across it, to provide Newport with a water supply. It was noted during the laying of the pipe that whenever a train passed over the bridge, the resulting oscillation 'had a range of several inches'. Charles Lindsay, an engineer who crossed the bridge by train a few days before the accident, commented on the 'bad treatment the bridge received from passing trains'.

Painters working on the bridge noticed a number of unusual things, not all of which they thought to mention at the time. Amongst these were a large number of iron bolts lying about, which for all they knew might have been left there by the builders. James Edward, questioned by the North British solicitors before the Inquiry, but not called to give evidence to the Court, spoke of having 'seen bolt heads falling about us when it was a frosty morning', he himself having been struck by one on the shoulder. 'One morning in particular while a train was going over three or four bolt heads came down altogether just beside me.' John Evans, similarly questioned, had 'found occasionally slack rivits [sic] or nuts awanting . . . Saw rivit holes without anything in them . . . Some of the diagonal bars were slack, one in particular was scarcely fastened at all. Several of them were worried by the motion of the bridge in high winds, or when a train passed over it. According to Evans, 'When trains came on the bridge it vibrated from side to side until the train was three to four girders from you, when she began to lift up and down as the motions became amalgamated like, and after she passed the same side to side motion was felt again.' Evans had experimented by tying a stone to the handrail so that it hung down, and 'watched its motion as a train came on and passed.'[93]

Maintaining the Bridge

Responsibility for maintaining the bridge once it had been handed over to the North British was to be shared. Bouch himself was engaged to look after the bridge at an annual fee of 100 guineas, and he in turn appointed Henry Noble as his inspector. Maintenance of the permanent way was the responsibility of James Bell, the North British engineer. Between them they had five staff. Noble had a boatman, whose job it was to examine the bridge from the water for three shillings and sixpence an hour; a lamplighter at one guinea a week; and a foreman. Bell had two men on the bridge to tighten the bolts on the fishplates and ensure that the rails were secure. All commentators testify to Noble's dedication to his job, but also to his lack of expertise when it came to ironwork. He was determined to keep the cost of maintenance to an absolute minimum. He instructed the lamplighter, McKinney, to go round turning off the twenty-eight gas lamps at 3.00 a.m. on summer mornings. He sometimes paid for materials to repair the bridge out of his own pocket. When it was discovered that by some oversight the contract to paint the bridge had not included the woodwork, some 87,000 cubic feet of it, he blandly suggested that if supplied with the paint, his men could do the work in and amongst their regular inspection duties. He became almost obsessively concerned with the effects of the scouring action of the water on the bridge supports, and arranged for thousands of tons of rubble to be laid around them. As a result, he was able to report, 'the heaviest train makes no perceptible motion below, and if it were not for the noise you would not believe a train had passed over'.

In March of 1879, Noble sent a diver down to examine the remains of the girder which had remained there ever since being blown off the piers in February of 1877. This inspection showed that the scour had dredged a great trough underneath the girder, and Noble decided to have the tieplates blown apart with dynamite, so that the remaining ironwork would collapse into the hole to be covered with rubble. There then followed an almost farcical episode, as he tried to secure the necessary explosive. 'In consequence of the dynamite agent at Dundee having no dynamite in his store,' he reported,

> I had to go personally with my man to the various quarries and beg it, and as there is a heavy penalty if it's known you are carrying it through a town, great secrecy had to be adopted. In fact very few persons know what we have been about, and I paid for everything in connection with the job in ready cash. It was the best and only method I could adopt to get over the affair quietly and economically.[94]

Conscientious he may have been, but this was no substitute for expert knowledge, and while Noble was certainly experienced in brickwork and masonry, he knew little about ironwork. This did not stop him from carrying out minor repairs himself. In October 1879, only weeks before the disaster, Noble heard a chattering noise in some of the tie bars as a train passed overhead. On investigation, he discovered that some of the bars had come loose, due to the slackening of the gib and cotter tensioning device. He then proceeded to purchase a quantity of iron from a local ironmonger, and from it cut 150 wedges to fill the gap. This dealt with the slackness, but he failed to realise that the loss of tension was due to the bending of the tie bolts within the lugs. According to Rapley, 'with the best of intentions Noble had unwittingly contributed to the fate of the bridge.'[95] Some defects he did report to Bouch, and when he found some deep vertical cracks in the cast-iron columns Bouch was told about it. Bouch's response was to comment that Brunel had had similar problems with his bridge at Chepstow, and gave orders for the defective parts to be braced with hoops of iron.[96]

CHAPTER 5

AFTER THE FALL

—⊷◆⊷—

FIRST REACTIONS

Madam,

Last night will be remembered in the history of Fife for all generations to come. None living in the North of Fife has yet seen or felt such a night the Great Tay Bridge is fallen, and the 7 o'clock train from Edinburgh is also down with it and all the passengers lost. And it is now very painful for me to say that David Cunningham is lost. By the deplorable Fall of the Tay-bridge he and a young lad from the Gauldry Ann Dewar Son Ann will know him they took the train from St Fort station to go to there work to the new Asylum near Lochee. I went to see the broken down bridge to find out about the trains knowing that David C was to cross. What a sight it is now the 12 large High Pillars with the High Girders is all down with all there Iron Works is now out of sight in the water . . . to know and think that your Neighbours and Acquaintances is laying in the cold Tay is very trying to flesh and blood.[97]

So wrote Angus Mackay in his distress to Miss Morison Duncan on Monday 29 December 1879. How many such letters must have been sent to bring the tragic news to households near and far. And of course for those with no personal line of communication, the local and national press were quick to publish what news there was, and send their newsmen and graphic artists in all haste to the scene to discover more. First accounts were inevitably brief. The correspondent in Monday's *Times* reported simply that:

Tonight a heavy gale swept over Dundee and a portion of the Tay Bridge was blown down while the train from Edinburgh was passing. It is believed that the train is in the water, but the gale is still so strong that a steamboat has not yet been able to reach the bridge. The scene at the Tay Bridge station is appalling. Many thousand persons are congregated around the buildings, and strong men and women are wringing their hands in despair.[98]

By the time this report appeared on the breakfast tables of the nation, the scene on the Tay was clear to watchers on the shore. The weather was now calm, and the surface of the river displayed no trace of the turbulence of the night before, but what it did show was the terrible gap where the High Girders had once stood. But what had happened to the train and its passengers? To a telegram from the Queen's private secretary, Sir Henry Ponsonby, expressing the royal dismay and asking for more information, the Provost could only pass on the erroneous information provided by the railway officials that nearly 300 passengers, as well as the servants of the company, were believed to have died. As to the causes of the disaster, Sir James Falshaw, deputy chairman of the North British, was quick to explain it as an act of God, and therefore

After the accident – the view of the bridge from the south.
Dundee City Library

the fault of no man. Few were inclined to agree with him, and the President of the Board of Trade announced the setting up of a Court of Inquiry that very day. By the time the newspapers had got over the initial shock of the tragedy, their approach to the question of blame was remarkably philosophical, and to the question of the rebuilding of the bridge remarkably positive. While recognising the central role and responsibility of Sir Thomas Bouch, few were prepared, at this stage at least, to cast him in the role of scapegoat. As the *Glasgow Evening Times* reflected,

> Sir Thomas Bouch had necessarily to use his own judgement in regard to points of novelty on which the experience of other engineers would give him but small assistance. His work, taking into account its surprising cheapness, had been universally pronounced a success, and there can be little doubt that it would in ordinary circumstances have become the parent of many similar structures. Encouraged by the Tay Bridge the engineers would have boldly essayed to answer the call of enterprising capitalists by offering to throw arches over any estuary, however wide. But it is inevitable that this accident should produce circumspection and caution.[99]

Closer to home, the *Dundee Courier* was even more bullish about the whole scheme, confident that the bridge would have to be rebuilt without delay (as indeed the senior officials of the North British had already privately decided) and anxious only that this time the bridge should carry a double track, since in addition to the operational advantages, 'it is clear that if we are to have an erection on which the public will venture their lives, it must be one of a broader base, of less height, and one less top heavy than that which was wrecked on Sunday evening.'[100]

The Search Begins

The rebuilding of the bridge would not even be begun for some years, and there were many more pressing matters to attend to first. Chief among them was to carry out a search for the remains of the victims, and a thorough investigation of the remains of the bridge and the train.[101]

Divers at work on the river bed in the search for the train.
Eduardo Alessandro Gallery

The search began at first light on the morning of the 29th, when the steam launch *Fairweather* made its way upstream to the bridge with harbourmaster Robertson on board, together with John Fox, a diver employed by the Harbour Trust. Fox was sent down at a point about thirty feet to the south of the third pier of the high girders, and from that point on the river bed he was able to see along the fallen girders in both directions until they were lost in the murk. There was no sign of the train.

When it became clear that for the time being the divers could do no more, the *Fairweather* was steamed along the line of the bridge, and an examination carried out of the piers which had supported the high girders. They were a sorry sight, with the iron columns snapped off and lying in a tangle on the broken stonework of the piers, though the brickwork of the piers in all cases was practically undamaged.

Shortly after eleven o'clock that same morning a second steamer, the *Forfarshire*, left the harbour to join in the search. On board it carried the Provost, James Cox, Dugald Drummond, and the brooding figure of Sir Thomas Bouch, as well as a number of officials of the North

British Company. For some hours it passed backwards and forwards along the line of the bridge, but found nothing.

At Taybridge Station orders had been given to prepare one of the refreshment rooms as a temporary mortuary. Outside the station, friends, relatives and bystanders waited in the gathering gloom for news, only to be told that there was no news, and that no bodies had yet been recovered. But in fact one had been. Late that evening, in shallow water further down the Fife coast, the body of a middle aged woman dressed in black was recovered by a mussel dredger, and conveyed to Dundee.[102] It was the body of Anne Cruickshank, Lady Baxter's house-maid, and the only one to be recovered for many days. On Tuesday the divers resumed their search. John Fox was once again sent down at the third pier of the high girders, and walked northwards along the fallen superstructure towards the fourth pier, discovering nothing new. For some reason Peter Harley, also employed by the Harbour Trust, was sent down at the same point and with the same result. Further to the Dundee side a diver engaged by the North British, Edward Simpson, dived by the sixth pier, where he discovered one of the spans lying on its side on the river bed, with its top facing downstream.

Pieces of wreckage being salvaged at Broughty Ferry. Some of the wood from the train was made into souvenirs of the disaster.
Eduardo Alessandro Gallery

One of the high girders revealed at low tide. Above it stands the remains of a cast-iron column on its foundation. *Dundee City Library*

In the afternoon of Tuesday, the train itself was sighted for the first time. Having twice drawn a blank in the area between the third and fourth piers, Fox now tried between the fourth and fifth. Here the girder, as elsewhere, was found lying on what had been originally its eastward facing side, but this time Fox found within it one of the carriages, unexpectedly standing upright but without its roof, and with extensive damage to both windows and doors. Within the carriage Fox could make our little except for some pieces of splintered wood and torn cushions. He was, however, able to retrieve some scraps of oilcloth which when brought to the surface identified his discovery as the first class carriage, which, in the original order of the coaches had been placed behind the third class carriage at the very front of the train.[103]

It was not perhaps surprising, given the strength of the current at this point in the river, that most moveable items had by now been sucked out of the train and carried downstream. In the whole course of the diving operation nothing in the way of personal belongings, and no bodies at all, were found to be inside the carriages. But downstream it was a different story, and the beach at Broughty Ferry, some four miles down the river on the Dundee side, became the repository for a melancholy collection of clothing and personal effects, which were quickly transferred for identification by relatives to the mortuary set up at Taybridge Station. Some were not difficult to identify – the caps of both the engine driver and his fireman; the basket belonging to the guard, David Johnston, with his flags still in it, neatly rolled. Johnston had not been on duty that night, but had been coming into Dundee ready to take his place on the first train out on the Monday morning. There was a handbag containing a collection of personal belongings, and there was the muff which had belonged to Jessie Bain.[104]

The discovery of all these items, and more especially their public display, can only have added to the distress of the relatives of the victims. By this stage, there can have been no realistic hope that anyone had survived the disaster, though how many of the relatives must have envied the good fortune of Mrs Upton, whose daughter Alice was be-lieved to have perished with the train, only for her to learn by telegram on the Tuesday that instead of travelling the girl had stayed overnight in Edinburgh, and would soon be home safe and well.

There could not be many miracles like that, and indeed there were to be no more, but those who mourned longed in their grief to receive the bodies of their relations into their care. Impatience with what *The Times* called the 'barrenness of the diving operations' resulted in the organisation of regular search parties on both sides of the river, but still the only finds were of debris from the train and the bridge, and more pathetic relics of the unfortunate passengers and crew.

The funeral of the only victim discovered so far, Ann Cruickshank, took place on Thursday 1 January, an occasion which brought out large crowds to pay their respects, and that same evening some boatmen out in the Tay found a second body, also female, but it eluded the grasp of their boathooks and sank out of sight. A fine tortoiseshell comb identified it as Jessie Bain. No more bodies were released by the river until the following Monday, eight days after the disaster, when David Johnston, the off-duty guard travelling on the train, was found. The next day, five more bodies were brought up, using grappling irons; James Leslie, a clerk in a timber firm, William Jack, a grocer, James Crichton, a ploughman, and Robert Watson, an iron moulder. In the evening they found the fireman of no. 224, John Marshall, his face ter-ribly burned from being hurled against the furnace. On the Wednesday there were six more; David Neish, a schoolmaster from Lochee, John

Sharp, a joiner, William Threlfall, a confectioner's apprentice, Walter Ness, a saddler, William Macdonald, a sawmiller from Blackness, and a flax dresser, James Miller. On the Thursday four more – Archie Bain, Thomas Davidson, Alexander Robertson, and James Henderson.[105]

The following week an unusual experiment was attempted in the search – a gullible shoemaker called Barclay enlisted the help of a female clairvoyant, and the pair of them set out in a small yacht across the water. Close by a large sandbar known as the Middle Bank, the woman claimed to have detected the body of a man in dark clothing, with a watch and some coins in his pockets. A trawl was put down, but the water was too deep for it to reach the bottom.[106]

And so it went on until by the end of January thirty-three bodies had been recovered. In later months more were to come to the surface from time to time – the last known being washed up on the shores of Caithness nearly four months after the accident. Thirteen were never found at all. Out on the water the diving operations continued, buoyed up by the discovery of the first-class carriage. On Wednesday, the last day of 1879, Fox went back down to the carriage, though he came across nothing new either then, or on a second dive some way

No. 224 after being recovered from the river bed. The engine was repaired and continued in service for many years.
St Andrews University, Valentine Collection

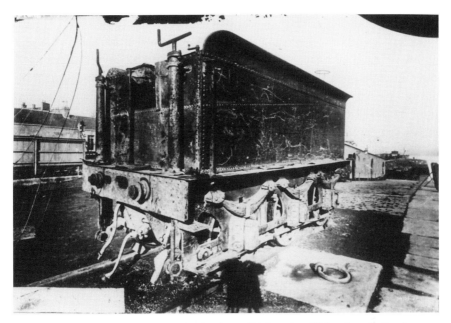

The tender after recovery. *St Andrews University, Valentine Collection*

further north. While he was down, however, Edward Simpson began to explore the section between piers four and five, where almost at once he discovered the third-class carriage which had been next to the engine. On his second dive, close to the fifth pier, he at last came across no. 224, lying on its side within the girder, but almost completely undamaged. Later inspection was to show that the throttle was open, and that the Westinghouse brake with which the train was fitted had not been applied. Clearly, for the driver of the train, the fall of the bridge had come with no warning.[107]

On Thursday, three divers went down – Fox, Simpson, and one John Barclay, engaged by the railway company – but none of them found anything of significance. On Friday the weather was too bad for diving, and on Saturday all that was found was a piece of handrail from a third-class carriage, a number of carriage roof lights, and part of the handrail from the bridge itself. A new diver, William Thoms, came across a fracture in the girder south of the fourth pier, but was ordered back to the shore before he could examine it properly. On Sunday a total of five divers went down, most of them to carry on with the search of the girders which held the train. Edward Simpson found the crack in the girder discovered the previous day by Thoms, estimating it to be about 18 inches wide, and also picked up a tail light from the rear of the guard's van. Thoms explored the first-class carriage and returned with more pieces of oilcloth and a couple of warming pans. The Harbour Trust had engaged a new diver, Charles Tate, and he began to examine, not the train, but the piers which had supported the columns under the high girders, and he found that part of the iron casing surrounding the concrete base of one of the piers had broken away, leaving the concrete exposed. More diving took place on the Monday, but without any material discoveries being made.[108]

THE RELIEF FUND

As the diving operations continued in that first week after the fall, and while the relatives waited for news, some progress was being made in arranging for relief for the bereaved. In an age when it was not expected that the state would step in and provide for those left destitute by the loss of a husband or father, it was expected that private charity would do something to cushion the blow, at least in the short term. On the Wednesday following the tragedy, the Town Council called a public meeting at which an account was given of the diving operations so far, and a proposal approved to set up a relief committee which would receive donations and 'administer the funds according to the necessities of the case'. Provost Brownlie was to chair the committee, and he was able to report that already the sum of £1,980 16s. had been donated, largely made up of £500 from the North British Company, a further £500 from the directors' own pockets, and £250 from Sir Thomas Bouch.[109]

In the course of time, requests were to come in to the Provost for money to relieve the distress and real hardship suffered by the dependents of those killed in the disaster. Few asked for themselves, but left it to some person of standing in the community – minister, doctor, or schoolmaster perhaps, to petition on their behalf. Thus Laura Davidson wrote from the Free Church manse in St Andrews on behalf of Mr and Mrs Sharp, the aged and infirm parents of John Sharp, their sole support before the accident. On 6 January, Aeneas Gordon, minister of Kettle parish church, interceded on behalf of Mrs Crichton, mother of James Crichton, ploughman. 'The circumstances of this poor woman,' he explained, 'are singularly sad. On Friday the 26th ulto. her husband, a ploughman in Downfield Farm was buried, he himself having died suddenly on Monday 22nd, while following his cart in the field. James her son came home from the Mains of Fintry with the intention of

returning early in the week to live with and provide for his mother and
sisters, some of whom are at present attending the Kettle School.' Thus
also Dr Boyd of St Andrews to Provost Brownlie:

> Dear Sir,
>   There is a poor creature here, a girl of twenty-two with
> a child ten weeks old, left a widow by the awful disaster. Her
> husband, a fine young fellow, walked away that evening to join
> the train at Leuchars. He was a cleaner in the employ of the
> railway company. Her father, Brand, has been twenty-eight
> years a driver in the company's service. They are all particu-
> larly decent. She is left with a child a burden on their parents.
> Her mother told me they should never want while the parents
> could support them, and they had not dropped a hint to me,
> tho' seeing them constantly, of any aid from the fund. But
> I have taken upon myself to bring the case before you, and
> I think a little help to provide mourning and the like, and
> generally give a lift to the poor girl, would be well bestowed.[110]

This approach on behalf of the cleaner's wife brought in a cheque
for £3.00, which even allowing for inflation seems not over generous.
Apparently Dr Boyd thought so too, as his letter of thanks contained a
further request that the Provost 'should consider the case favourably.'
But of course there were other and no less urgent pleas for assistance.
A small donation was supplied to Robert Henderson, the aged grand-
father of another of the bridge's victims, young James Smith, who had
been in the habit of visiting the old man in Springfield and taking him
a few comforts. Indeed he had been coming home to Dundee after just
such an errand when the bridge fell. Money was found for the mother
of David Watson, and the aged parents of Annie Spence.[111]

The sums disbursed to the relatives of the victims were generally
small, and in no sense were intended to provide long-term support.
For this they had to look to the North British for compensation, and it
would appear that the company met its obligations in this respect. 'It
is so far consoling to know', commented a newspaper account on the
anniversary of the disaster,

> that those whose breadwinners were carried down with the
> train were not left to face chill penury as an aggravation of

their woe. The spontaneous generosity of the public provided a fund to relieve their immediate wants, and the North British Railway Company have acknowledged their responsibility by meeting the claims made against them. Almost all these claims have now been arranged, and the Railway Company deserves praise for their liberal treatment of the families of the officials of the ill-fated train, who have been dealt with on the same scale as the passengers, though legally the Company were not bound to make any settlement in their case.[112]

One is less impressed with the generosity of the North British when it is discovered that having settled most of the claims for compensation, the Company proceeded to ask for their contribution to the relief fund to be returned, as did the directors. In the end, out of donations totalling £6,527, less than £2,000 was spent on relief, most of the balance being sent back to the subscribers. What could not be returned was retained in the fund, which was ultimately wound up after transferring the accumulated balance to the Piper Alpha Disaster Appeal in 1988. Not that the bill for compensation was as much as it might have been either. As *The Times* commented with satisfaction, 'Fortunately for the North British Railway Company no one holding a high position lost his life, and in consequence the compensation claims were very small and settled without difficulty.'[113]

THE SALVAGE OPERATION

While some relief was being found for the relatives and dependents of the dead, the work of salvaging the remains of the train and the bridge continued. Bouch was still officially the engineer in charge of the bridge, and he appointed contractors to raise the fallen girders from the river bed using giant pontoons originally intended for what would have been his next great venture – the building of the bridge across the Forth. Not everything went smoothly. The girders were too big to be raised in one piece and had to be cut into manageable sections with dynamite. In an attempt to raise the fourth high girder complete with the second class carriage still trapped inside it, an explosive charge designed to free the girder damaged and sank one of the lifting pontoons. There were problems too with the engine, which Dugald Drummond was particularly anxious to recover. The plan was to lift it with pontoons and tow it to the beach at Tayport, and indeed this was done, but not before it had twice broken the lifting chains, and sunk to the bottom again. Remarkably it had suffered only superficial damage – and most of that from the lifting operation rather than from the fall. Drummond was able to report to the North British directors with some satisfaction that 'The engine is very slightly damaged, and it will not cost more than £50 to put it in working condition. With the exception of the left hand trailing axle-bar, which has a small portion of the outer end broken, the tender is not in any way injured, and this damage will not prevent it from being serviceable.'[114] In fact no. 224 was soon to be back on the rails, and continued in service for another thirty years.

CHAPTER 6

COURT OF INQUIRY

————◆————

THE COURT CONVENES

A Court of Inquiry had been set up by Lord Sandon, the President of the Board of Trade, with commendable speed. Its instructions were that it was to hold a formal investigation into the causes of and the circumstances attending the accident to the Tay Bridge, Dundee, on Sunday 28 December, 1879, and it is worth pointing out that these instructions made no mention of allocating blame. The Court consisted of three men, Henry Rothery, the chairman and official Commissioner for Wrecks, Colonel William Yolland, the Chief Inspector for Railways, and William Henry Barlow, a professional engineer and also the current President of the Institution of Civil Engineers. Henry Law was appointed as engineering adviser to the Board of Trade, and Dr William Pole, the current Secretary to the Institution, as technical adviser to Bouch.

The Commissioners wasted little time in coming to Dundee, and the first sitting of the Court took place on the morning of Saturday, 3 January, 1880, in the city courthouse. The three principal interested parties – the Board of Trade, the North British Railway Company, and Bouch himself – had each engaged legal counsel, with Mr Trayner representing the Board, Mr J.B. Balfour the Company, and Mr George Bidder, Sir Thomas. The chairman began the proceedings by explaining the purpose of the preliminary hearing – to establish the 'mere surrounding facts which may be locally ascertained'. More specifically he wanted to find out just what had happened on the night of the disaster, and also to establish the condition of the girders and the train, now lying on the bed of the river. He then adjourned the hearing until 2.00 p.m. to allow the Court to visit the scene of the disaster.[115]

The proceedings were resumed on the afternoon of Saturday, and continued on the Monday and Tuesday of the following week. The first group of witnesses to be heard were those employees of the railway who had been involved in the events of the 28th and had lived to tell the tale. These were the men whose accounts of the loss of the train have been told and retold on countless occasions since – Thomas Barclay, the signalman, and his friend John Watt; Henry Somerville, the signalman from the north box; stationmaster Smith from Taybridge Station; the stationmaster, ticket collector and porter from St Fort. But the picture that emerged from their accounts, clear enough in some particulars, left many questions unanswered. Not one of them had actually seen the train fall, and at best they could only speak of sudden flashes from the bridge, disappearing riding lights, and dark shapes in the murk. What they could agree on was at the time of its disappearance the train had not long entered the high girders, and their evidence on this point had already indicated to the diving parties where to begin their search.

Having questioned the employees of the railway company, the Court also heard from some members of the public who had been eyewitnesses of the tragedy – Alexander Maxwell, and the Clark brothers, George and William. Next came testimony as to the weather at the time of the fall – the scientific observations of Admiral Dougall and Captain Scott of the *Mars*, and the account of William McKelvie, superintendent of cemeteries in Dundee. According to McKelvie, the wind that had destroyed the bridge had also blown down eight or nine monuments in Balgay cemetery, and fifteen in the Eastern. No previous gale in his experience had done as much damage.

The last group of witnesses, the divers themselves, could add only a certain amount of information to this account, and that incomplete and confused. The problem, as we have seen, was a combination of appalling working conditions and poor overall direction of diving operations, but some facts could nevertheless be ascertained with some certainty, of which the most important was the position and disposition of the engine and its carriages. With this preliminary phase of the Inquiry completed, the Court was adjourned until some future date to be determined.[116]

THE PRECOGNITIONS

As it turned out the Inquiry was not to be resumed until February, and solicitors and agents for both the Board and the Company used the intervening period to track down witnesses and secure their testimony in the form of 'precognitions'. Not unnaturally each side tended to select for the hearings only those witnesses whose evidence would do no damage to their cause. Thus the evidence of David Young, Albert Grothe's boatman, described by Thornton as 'a conceited vainglorious man', would have been extremely damaging, if allowed to come out at the Inquiry. In the course of conversation in the solicitor's office, he made such remarks as 'The management of affairs at building the Bridge was extremely loose, and strict attention was not given to the construction and testing of the work…the iron was bad…ill made and deficient in quality . . . The concrete was not properly hardened . . . Mr Bouch's examination of the work was very cursory.' The evidence already referred to of James Edward, a painter with a grudge against the North British Company for refusing him the contract to repaint the bridge, would, if it had come to court, have alleged that there had been bad workmanship in the fixing of rivets and bolts in the ironwork of the girders and columns.[117]

The precognition of W.B. Thomson, proprietor of the famous Caledon shipyard on the Tay, likewise remained unproduced in court, but this time surely out of inadvertence rather than design. Thomson had been to church in Broughty Ferry on the Sunday of the fall, and had emerged into the storm a few minutes after seven o'clock. He had walked down to the beach, but the force of the wind had prevented him from getting right down to the sea front, and he had taken shelter at the corner of James Place. 'While there,' he told Thornton,

> I distinctly saw two luminous columns of mist or spray travel-
> ling across the river in the direction of the wind. Another one
> formed in front of me just in an instant. It appeared to rise from
> the centre of the river. I never saw anything like this before,
> and looked round to see if anyone was near me, but seeing
> nobody thought it was better to take shelter. I went inside
> the railings in front of James Place, and held on by one of
> them thinking that the column, which was advancing towards
> me, was to carry everything before it. It passed over me. It
> was spray from the river, not solid water. It struck the house
> behind me with a hissing noise. The height of each of these
> columns was I should think 250 to 300 feet . . . My theory
> is that the north end of the bridge gave way first, the failure
> being caused by one such column rising or passing under it.
> Such a thing would tend to raise the girders from their piers,
> thereby overcoming part of the resistance offered to the lateral

pressure of the wind. My theory put briefly is that there was a heavy upwards pressure as well as a lateral pressure in the wind that night. I never saw anything like it.[118]

Thomson's theory, well founded or not, was at least in line with the Company's argument that the weather was the real culprit, and it is surprising that Thornton did not see fit to call him on his clients' behalf. But Thornton was perhaps preoccupied with trying to find witnesses who would help him rebut the evidence of another equally prominent witness - former Provost William Robertson, who was anxious to make public his conviction that on many occasions when he had travelled over the bridge, the driver had greatly exceeded the recommended 25 mph speed limit, and that the drivers regularly tried to race the ferry across the Tay in the mornings. He had often, he claimed, 'heard the passengers twitting the driver that the Boat would race him this morning . . . I believe there was a wager made that the Boat would land its passengers first four mornings in one week. That week I thought the speed was very fast.' By way of contradiction, Thornton had also interviewed one Frank Whitehurst, an upholsterer, who asserted that he had often travelled with Robertson, and had never known him complain of the speed. Whitehurst, however, refused to give evidence, and the North British, unlike the Board of Trade, had no power to compel him to do so. After recording Robertson's precognition therefore, Thornton wrote to Adam Johnstone, chief solicitor for the North British, in Edinburgh to warn him of the danger, and advised him to have 'two good and experienced engine drivers present who were in the practice of driving over the bridge, and would be able to say that they never exceeded speed, and never observed anything calling for remark or observation, and never felt any tremor or oscillation.'[119]

THE INQUIRY RESUMES

When the Inquiry resumed on 26 February, Robertson duly produced his story, claiming that he had once timed the train at nearly 43 mph, after which experience he had abandoned his season ticket and gone back to using the ferry. His complaints of excessive speed were supported by John Leng, proprietor of the *Advertiser*, and by other prominent citizens of Dundee. Against them was called one Henry Quosbarth, the German Consul, who asserted that he also had travelled regularly across the bridge, but had never done so at 40 mph, and had never experienced the slightest discomfort or anxiety. Stationmaster Smith was called, and was able to say that he had looked into Mr Robertson's complaints, but had been unable to find any evidence to back them up. Not two but seven engine drivers were called, all of whom were adamant that they never exceeded the 25 mph speed limit, and that the crossing never took less than five and a half or six minutes. Allegations that the train on occasion used to race the ferry across the estuary were vigorously denied.[120]

And so the debate on the question of excessive speeds remained inconclusive. Much more damaging to the bridge-makers, however, was the evidence soon to emerge about the Wormit Foundry, and the tale of mismanagement, poor workmanship, and lax supervision which that evidence would reveal. The chief witness for this stage of the hearing was the foundry foreman, Fergus Ferguson, a self-regarding and complacent young man, who made the mistake of saying to Rothery, of the work of the foundry, 'if I tried to explain it to you without you being a practical man you could never understand it'. Almost everything Ferguson said to the Court confirmed his lack of professionalism and good sense. He had taken it upon himself to decide on the thickness of the cast iron columns, regardless of his instructions. He contradicted himself repeatedly over the question of 'burning on' new lugs on columns where the original casting had been defective, and whether the process produced as strong a result as a properly cast column. His original estimate that he had had to break up some thirty or forty columns for defects in the casting became, under questioning from Trayner, something around two hundred. It soon became clear that for all his protestations he had failed to monitor the use of 'beaumont egg' to fill in blowholes in sub-standard castings. Of the casting iron itself, 'he wouldn't like to say it was the best, but as a general rule for building work it was not what you'd call terribly bad iron.'[121]

That Ferguson had got away with such inadequate workmanship for so long was due in turn to poor management by the contractors. Originally the foundry had been managed by its designer, Frank Beattie, a reasonably well-qualified and experienced engineer who had, or so he claimed, tried to persuade his employers to use better quality metal for the castings, but without success. Beattie was succeeded by Gerard Camphuis, a Dutchman formerly in the employ of de Bergue's, who had been brought in because of his supposed expertise in driving piles for the bridge foundations, and had never before managed a foundry. Trayner ran rings round him, and by persistent questioning soon discredited his claim that despite his lack of experience he could 'judge very well of foundry work'. The overall impression gained by this stage of the inquiry was of a foundry managed by incompetent and complacent staff, producing dangerously defective ironwork which had in fact failed to meet the test imposed upon it.[122]

After this interrogation of witnesses as to the affairs of the foundry, the Court turned to the question of maintenance. Here the key witness was the unhappy Henry Noble, formerly Bouch's assistant in charge of the brickwork of the bridge, but since its completion the inspector of the Tay Bridge, in sole charge of all of the structure apart from the rails themselves.

Noble's lack of qualifications for this responsible position were soon all too apparent. All he knew about was brickwork. He had begun his career as an apprentice bricklayer, and having served his time was employed by the Board of Works for nine years before being promoted to an inspector by the Metropolitan Board. As he freely admitted, he had no skills as an engineer, and no experience of ironwork. Yet here he now was, the inspector of a bridge of which five-sixths of the columns and all of the superstructure were made of iron. To carry out his duties, Noble had been given no instructions, a staff of seven (later reduced to three) and a small steamer, the *Tay Bridge*. Trayner had a field day. Having established that Noble had no experience of ironwork, and had been taken on by Bouch in 1871 as an inspector of brickwork only, he turned to Noble's responsibilities with regard to the bridge:

– Then when you were taken on by the Company, I understand that your duties were to see whether or not there was any scouring at the bottom of the piers?
– Yes.
– Those were your special duties?
– Those were my special duties.
– They were in fact your only duties.
– They were the only duties I had really to perform.
– You said that you generally made your inspections in September and March.
– My soundings.
– What did you do at other times?
– I would go over the columns of the bridge.

– You were not appointed to do that.
– No, I know that.

On the question of what instructions Noble had received from the Company, Trayner asked:

– You never received instructions from them to report any default that you should discover in the structure of the bridge?
– No, I never had any such instructions.
– Had you general instructions to repair anything you might find defective without going to a superior in the company's service?
– I never had any instructions at all . . .

'So far as you know,' Trayner persisted, 'there was no one there charged at all with the duty of looking after the ironwork?'

– Not underneath the platform, but above there was.
– No one was there to look after the ironwork of the bridge as far as it stood between the top of the pier and the bottom of the platform?
– Except myself.
– You had no instructions.
– I had no instructions.
– Did any engineer make periodic visits to the bridge on behalf of the company? Was there a stated time, once a fortnight or once a week or once a month when any engineer came to look at the bridge and give it an overhaul?
– No.
– Did no one inspect the bridge from the time you went there, which was in May 1878, till its fall in December, 1879?
– No one but me.
– No one was there to judge the effect of the loosening of these bars or the proper measure to be taken to remedy these defects but yourself?
– Nobody but myself.
– Did you tell Sir Thomas Bouch at any time that you had heard this chattering of the bars, and what you had done?
– No, I never told him.

What he lacked in know-how, Noble made up in dedication. He examined the iron columns and discovered in several of them great long cracks which he did report to Bouch, and Bouch gave orders for them to be strapped round with iron. Likewise he found cracks in the masonry of a number of piers, and these too were repaired with iron strapping. He examined the foundations below water level and discovered that the scour of the river had gouged out great depressions – he had them filled with rubble. He inspected the tie-bars bracing the columns and found many of them loose, so he bought seven shillings worth of iron with his own money and used it to pack the loose ties, almost certainly fixing them permanently out of position.[123]

The next important witness was Albert Grothe, the man who had been largely responsible for the construction of the bridge, and who had been at pains, on so many occasions in the past, to quieten fears in the public mind about its strength and stability. To give him his due Grothe was willing to admit that there might have been some examples of poor workmanship, and that 'in a large work like this, where there were 600 or 700 men employed, and with all materials floating in barges, it was impossible to keep so strict an eye on everything personally, as it would be in the same sort of work on shore.' On the other hand he was confident that no cast-iron work was used in the bridge which had not passed at least a visual inspection, and he had given positive instructions on the point to Camphuis. Neither he nor Camphuis, he had to concede, were experienced foundry men, but had left the technical foundry work to Ferguson.

But he could not so easily disclaim responsibility for his earlier assurances that the bridge was more than capable of withstanding the severest storm ever known on the Tay, nor did he try. When asked for his opinion about the cause of the fall, he responded that in his view it had been brought about by the sheer force of the wind, and he freely acknowledged that his earlier view on wind pressures had been mistaken. 'I see in my lecture,' he confessed, 'that I stated that the greatest wind that could ever be expected in this country was such a one as that in which the *Royal Charter* [sic] went down, when the pressure was 21 lbs per square foot, and upon that calculation I pointed out that the stability of the bridge was undoubted.'[124]

But had the bridge been designed to withstand even this much pressure from the wind, and what steps had its designer taken to ascertain the likely wind pressure in the Tay estuary? The court now turned to question Sir George Airy, the Astronomer Royal, who had been consulted on the subject of wind pressure in 1873, when Bouch was drawing up his plans for the projected bridge over the Forth. The full text of Airey's opinion was read out in court. 'We know,' Airy had written, 'that upon very limited surfaces, and for very limited times, the pressure of the wind does amount to sometimes 40 lbs per square foot, or in Scotland to probably more. However, I think we can say that the greatest wind pressure to which a plane surface like that of the bridge will be subjected to on its whole extent will be 10 lbs per square foot.'

In Airy's view, occasional or localised gusts, or 'irregular swirlings of the air', which might exert a pressure of 40 or 50 lbs per square foot on limited portions of the bridge, were unlikely to have any effect on the structure as a whole. In his opinion 50 lbs was probably the greatest pressure exerted by any wind in Britain in recent years, though he had no idea what the wind pressure might have been on the night the bridge fell, as there were no instruments for measuring it in Dundee at the time. Not altogether helpfully, he observed that at its height the storm had registered not more than 10lbs per square foot at his residence at Greenwich. Since the bridge had fallen, he had written a paper on winds that had apparently blown down bridges, and advised for the future that 'all calculations for the strength of a proposed structure should be based on the assumption of 120 lbs per square foot.' If it was in fact true that 50 lbs was the highest pressure likely to be reached in practice, a figure of 120 lbs seemed like overkill.[125]

Airy was followed by a rather more credible authority on meteorology – a professor from Cambridge called Stokes, who lectured the court on wind speed of up to 90 miles per hour, and pressures in excess of 50 lbs per square foot. Nor should they think of gusts of that speed being of only momentary duration – 'sometimes they will go on for two or three minutes, blowing very heavily indeed.' Next came Mr Henry Scott, Secretary to the Meteorological Council, who supported Mr Stokes in every particular. Certainly, he confirmed, winds in the Tay valley could reach the speeds and pressures Stokes had mentioned, and they could exert their force along a wide front, perhaps as much as 250 feet. The picture of a bridge which would be unaffected by sudden gusts of wind was beginning to look less and less plausible.[126]

All this served as an essential backcloth to the main event of the Inquiry – the examination of the bridge's designer, Sir Thomas Bouch.

Bouch up to this point had remained apparently unaffected by the Inquiry, and had busied himself since the disaster with planning the bridge over the Forth, and even the repair of the Tay Bridge. But he can hardly have been by this stage unaware that his professional reputation was now very much at stake, not just in terms of his competence as a designer, but also in terms of the lack of supervision he appeared to have exercised over both the construction and the maintenance of the bridge. His ordeal lasted for a day and a half – the whole of Friday 30th April, and the morning of the following Monday. He answered more than eight hundred questions put to him by counsel and the three members of the Court, and he staunchly defended not only his own reputation but also those of his colleagues and employees, and made not the slightest attempt to pass any blame on to them. Henry Noble, he assured the Court, was 'one of the best examiners of concrete and Portland cement I have come across in my experience, and one of the most careful.' He was full of praise for Allan D. Stewart, his technical assistant, who had done most of the calculations for the bridge design, and who, as Bouch freely acknowledged, had better qualifications as a mathematician than his master. Nevertheless, Bouch assured the Court, the calculations of girder load carried out by Stewart had all been done on Bouch's instructions.

Nor would he accept any criticism of the type of bridge he had chosen for the Tay – a design which he had used successfully on previous occasions, as in the Deepdale and Belah Viaducts. As for the cracks which had been discovered in the cast-iron columns, they had not caused him any great concern, and he had been informed that other notable bridge builders, including Brunel, had had similar problems but without any serious consequences. He had his own explanation for the disaster: 'that it was caused by the capsizing of one of the last or the two last carriages – that is to say the second-class carriage and the van; that they canted over against the girder.' Asked if that would have been enough to have destroyed the bridge, he responded, 'I have no doubt of it. Practically the first blow would be the momentum of the whole train until the couplings broke. If you take the body of the train going at that rate, it would destroy anything.' Yet he had to admit that in designing the bridge he had made no special allowance for wind pressure, and that admission alone was enough to ensure that he would leave the court with his professional reputation damaged beyond repair.[127]

One of the carriages found lying inside the girder. *Roland Paxton*

THE VERDICT

The Report of the Court of Inquiry was presented to both Houses of Parliament in June, 1880. Unusually it took the form of two separate documents. The first of these, signed only by Yolland and Barlow, set out the facts of the case as revealed by the evidence before the Court, and made no attempt to ascribe blame or responsibility to anyone. The second report was written by Rothery, without the acquiescence of his two colleagues, but in which the pronoun 'we' was used throughout, giving the impression that it represented the views of all three. This document was damning, and if it was critical of many of the protagonists in the affair, it damned Sir Thomas Bouch in particular.

In their report, Barlow and Yolland concentrated on the failure of the supports of the bridge – in particular the cast-iron columns and their wrought-iron cross ties – and considered their deficiencies in terms of design, manufacture and construction. The key design issue was of course wind pressure, and the extent to which the designers had taken wind pressure into account. The report rehearsed in detail the evidence on wind pressure provided by the experts, and by Bouch and Stewart. It noted also that in the great majority of railway structures no special provision for wind pressure was required, 'since the weight and lateral strength imparted to such structures in providing for the strains due to dead weight and load is more than sufficient to meet any lateral wind pressures which can arise'. Bouch, they noted, 'having provided amply for dead weight and moving loads in the Tay Bridge . . . did not consider it necessary to make special provision against wind pressure.'

In the information which they, through Bouch, provided to the Court, Dr Pole and Allan D. Stewart had claimed that in designing the bridge, a maximum pressure of 20 lbs of wind pressure was assumed, plus the usual margin of safety.[128] Taking this figure, and using it to calculate the stress on the cross ties, Barlow and Yolland reckoned that the ultimate strength of the ties should have been 45.88 tons. In theory, given the tensile strength of the iron used, and the cross-section of the ties, they should have been capable of bearing a load of 32.5 tons. But tests carried out for the Inquiry by Mr Kirkaldy showed that none of the ties tested came near to either of these figures. The mean ultimate strength of six ties tested without being attached to cast-iron lugs was only 25.6 tons, and of those attached to lugs, 24.1 tons. Moreover, 'Mr Kirkaldy's experiments show that the stretching or elongation of the ties, when tested with their fastenings, was greatly in excess of that due to elastic action of that material; a result attributable to the small bearing surfaces of the pins, gibs and cotters, and to the conical holes in the lugs.'

Similarly, with regard to the cast-iron lugs themselves, the tensile strength of the metal used for the lugs averaged 9.1 tons, yet in tests designed to simulate the stresses *in situ*, even sound lugs failed at less than 3 tons. 'We believe,' the report went on, 'this great apparent reduction of strength in the cast iron is attributable to the nature of the fastenings, which caused the stress to be brought on the edges or outer sides of the lugs instead of acting fairly upon them.'

On the general question of wind pressure, then, and the ability of the bridge to withstand the force of an extreme gale, Barlow and Yolland concluded that if the cross-bracing had been made strong enough, then the stability of the bridge against overturning should have been sufficient to resist a wind force of 40 lbs pressure. Yet as they observed, the storm which occurred on the night of 28 December 1879 was recorded on board the *Mars* training ship, lying near Newport, as between 10 and 11 on the Beaufort scale, and was especially characterised by strong gusts at intervals. By this stage, some loosening of the ties had already taken place, as discovered by Henry Noble, and cracks had already appeared in some of the cast-iron columns.

> In this state of the columns and ties, the storm of the 28th December 1879 occurred, which would necessarily produce great tension in the ties, varying as the heavy gusts bore upon different parts of the bridge; and when under these strains the train came on the viaduct bringing a large surface of wind pressure to bear, as well as increased weight on the piers, and accompanied by the jarring action due to its motion along the rails, the final catastrophe occurred.[129]

The second report, written by Rothery, came to broadly similar conclusions as to the defects of the structure and the causes of the fall. Where it differed was in its unequivocal attribution of blame. 'It seemed to me,' wrote Rothery, 'that we ought not to shrink from the duty however painful it might be, of saying with whom the responsibility for this casualty rests . . . I do not understand my colleagues to differ from me in thinking that the chief blame for this casualty rests with Sir Thomas Bouch, but they consider it is not for us to say so.' Rothery felt no such compunction.

> The conclusion then to which we have come, is that this bridge was badly designed, badly constructed, and badly maintained, and that its downfall was due to inherent defects in the structure which must sooner or later have brought it down. Sir Thomas Bouch is, in our opinion, mainly to blame . . . For the faults in design . . . he was entirely responsible. For the faults in construction . . . he was principally responsible. For the faults in maintenance . . . he was principally if not entirely responsible.

The bulk of Rothery's report was to substantiate these conclusions. The principal design fault, as he saw it, was in Bouch's failure to make any allowance for wind pressure on the structure. There was no real excuse for this failure, and even if Bouch had had no accurate information about wind pressures in the Tay estuary, nevertheless he ought to have been aware that it was common practice in France for bridge designers to build in an allowance of 55 lbs, and in the United States an allowance of 50 lbs per square foot. It was unfortunate, furthermore, that Bouch had not taken more care to ascertain the true character of the river bed before embarking on the design of the columns and foundations, and if it was argued that he had been misled by the borers, 'what right,' Rothery demanded, 'had Sir Thomas Bouch in a matter of such importance to trust solely to the word of the borers?' No suggestion was offered as to how Bouch might have checked those findings.

As for the Wormit Foundry, the great lack was of proper supervision. Once again Rothery found Bouch very much to blame.

> Sir Thomas Bouch seems to have left it to Hopkins, Gilkes & Co.; they left it to Mr Grothe, and he left it to Fergus Ferguson. With such supervision, or rather, we should say with the absence of all supervision, we can hardly wonder that the columns were not cast as perfectly as they should have been, and that fatal defects in the lugs and bolt-holes should not have been pointed out.

Yet if Bouch was to be awarded the lion's share of blame, there was still plenty to go round. 'We think also,' wrote Rothery,

> that Messrs Hopkins, Gilkes & Co. are not free from blame for having allowed such grave irregularities to go on at Wormit foundry . . . The Railway Company also are not free from blame for having allowed the trains to run through the High Girders at a speed greatly in excess of that which General Hutchinson had suggested as the extreme limit.

In addition to the question of blame, Rothery also addressed the central issue of cause, and here again he differed from the report of his two colleagues in that he gave considerable attention to Bouch's claim that the bridge had been brought down, not by the force of the wind, but by the action of the train in coming into contact with the girders. It was not, however, a theory that appealed to Rothery. If the train had brought down the bridge, he argued, then the girders at the south end of the navigations spans, within which the train and carriages had been found, should have fallen first. While evidence on this point was admittedly inconclusive, what indications there were pointed to the northern spans having been the first to collapse. Marks or scrapes found on the eastern girders by Bouch's assistant, Charles Meik, and which

The roof of one of the carriages on the platform at Taybridge Station. The diagonal gash across it was probably caused by its coming into contact with the top of the girder as they entered the water together. *Roland Paxton*

Bouch had claimed were proof of his theory that the last two carriages had canted over against the side of the bridge, were too superficial to account for the collapse.

So in the end Rothery's explanation of the accident was little different from that of his fellow members of the Court. 'What probably occurred,' he wrote,

> is this: the bridge had probably been strained, partly by the great speed at which the trains going northward were permitted to run through the High Girders. The result would be that owing to the defects, to which we have called attention, the wind ties would be loosened; so that when the gale of 28th December came on, a racking motion would be set up between the two triangular groups into which the six columns forming each pier were divided.
>
> Add to this the motion of a great weight of a moving train, and the strain on girders, columns and piers was suddenly too much for the structure to bear. Train, girders, piers and all had collapsed into the river, and if the exact sequence of events and the precise causes of the collapse would never be known to the full, the result was essentially and tragically the same.[130]

CHAPTER 7

THE REASON WHY

—◆—

In their two reports, the members of the Court of Inquiry had addressed two separate but related issues – what had caused the bridge to fall; and who was to blame? On the first point, the report signed by the two engineers, Barlow and Yolland, had been clear and unequivocal – that the cross-bracing on the cast-iron columns had been insufficiently strong to withstand the force of the gale. This was in the first instance a fault of design, though possibly exacerbated by failures of management and workmanship. In Rothery's view, as we have seen, these failures pointed the finger of blame principally at Bouch, both as the designer and as the overall supervisor of the project.

Yet not all contemporaries, nor all subsequent commentators, have agreed with these conclusions. Over the years there has developed a lively debate both on the causes of the bridge's failure, and on the attribution of blame or moral responsibility for that event. These issues may now seem academic, but at the time they were of great practical importance, in that they would have a direct bearing on the design of the new Tay Bridge, and even on the design of the bridge over the Firth of Forth.

WHAT CAUSED THE FALL?

Both at the time and in subsequent years differences of opinion as to the cause or causes of the disaster have arisen. Indeed no sooner had the President of the Board of Trade, Lord Sandon, announced the setting up of a Court of Inquiry, than the Board was inundated with letters from members of the public offering their explanations of the calamity. Some of these contributions were engagingly dotty, some blatantly vindictive, and several well-informed and constructive.

'It may be found,' suggested one Elisabeth Dean, 'that electricity has been the cause of the destruction of the Tay Bridge.' What she seems to have had in mind was that 'The iron of the bridge could have

95

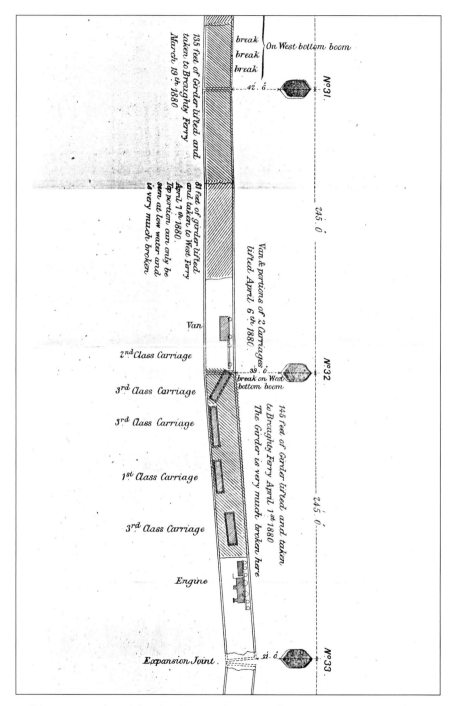

Diagram produced for the Court of Inquiry showing the position of the engine and the carriages on the river bed. *British Rail*

become during the cold weather a strong negative. In the journey from Edinburgh the train by friction would have collected much electricity thus becoming positive and the living bodies of the passengers being positive too, then when the centre of the bridge was arrived at, this frictional electricity would upset the electrical equilibrium.' W.E. Surtees, writing to Rothery, smelled corruption. He had owned a few shares in Hopkins, Gilkes & Co., but the company had gone into liquidation as a direct result of involvement in the Tay Bridge venture. Surtees had found out that the company had been promoted by one Joseph Dodds, MP, who had been associated with a number of fraudulent concerns. Moreover he had discovered that Bouch also had a considerable investment in Hopkins, Gilkes & Co., and he managed to suggest that the work had been skimped deliberately in order to put money into Bouch's own pocket. E. Talbot, however, as a manufacturer with long experience of the iron trade, directed the attention of the Inquiry more usefully to the quality of the iron used in the bridge construction. He was aware that iron made in the Middlesbrough district, as the Tay Bridge iron had been, commonly 'partook of what we in the Iron Trade call a "cold shut" property, and is therefore ill adapted to bear an unusual strain upon it.' James Murray anticipated the views of many subsequent commentators when he expressed a 'firm conviction, after taking into consideration the great length and height of the bridge . . . with the plan thereof, that of necessity the bridge had an oscillating tendency, especially when great or extreme pressure was brought to bear thereon. Such pressure came on 28th December last in the form of a giant hurricane bearing furiously and with tremendous force on the bridge broadside.'[131]

In considering all the explanations of the bridge failure which have been advanced, there remain essentially two schools of thought – those who argue that the bridge was brought down by the train, which either canted over against the side of the girders, or actually left the track, and those who believe that the bridge itself collapsed under the force of the storm, taking the train down with it. A variation on the first view – that the train brought down the bridge – is the suggestion that over time the passage of trains over the bridge caused cumulative damage to the fabric of the bridge in the form of metal fatigue in the cast-iron fixings of the columns. It was therefore only a matter of time before a disaster happened. Against that there are those who argue that the key issue was wind pressure, and the failure of the designers to make adequate

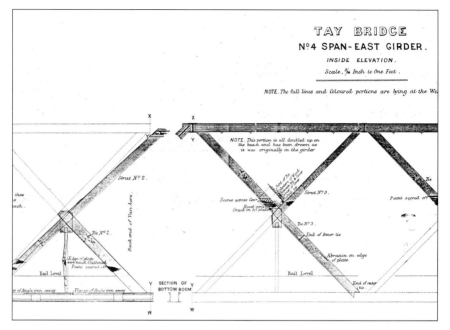

Diagram produced for the Inquiry, showing the score marks on no. 4 girder, which Bouch believed would prove that the train brought down the bridge.
British Rail

allowance for the kind of gale-force winds not uncommon along the Tay estuary. Put simply, the bridge blew down. A very common view amongst contemporaries, and still popular today, was that the additional wind resistance provided by the presence of the train on the bridge at the fateful time was a major contributory factor in the collapse. As it was the cast-iron columns supporting the girders which collapsed, attention has also focused then and since on possible weaknesses in the metal of the columns, arising from poor quality iron, or poor quality control of the casting process, or both.

The leading proponent of the first theory was of course Bouch himself, who remained firmly convinced until his death that the collapse of the bridge had been brought about by one or both of the last two coaches, the second-class carriage and the guard's van, leaning over under the force of the gale, and smashing into the east side of the girder, snapping the ties, and causing the whole column to fail. So sure was he that examination of girder no. 4, still sunk on the river bed, would prove his theory that he stayed on in Dundee until the last minute, waiting for it to be raised, before having to leave to face the

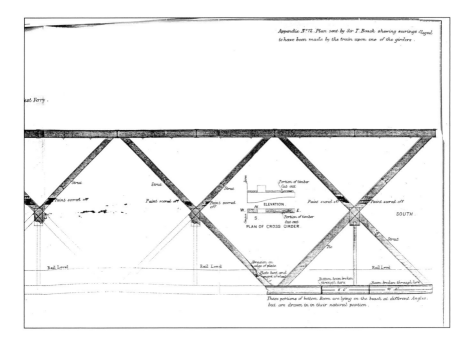

Appendix No. 12. Plan sent by Sir T. Bouch shewing scorings alleged to have been made by the train upon one of the girders.

Court of Inquiry, now moved to London, on 17 April. Unfortunately for Bouch, he was thwarted by Dugald Drummond, the locomotive superintendent, who insisted on raising the engine first.[132]

Bouch's theory was supported, perhaps not surprisingly, by his assistant, Allan D. Stewart, and by Dr Pole, a distinguished mathematician brought in as an independent expert. In their evidence to the Inquiry they suggested that the train hit the high girders, and the shock was transmitted to the piers, which fractured and brought the bridge down. There were a number of possible objections to this theory. While it was true that scrape marks on girder No. 4 gave some colour to this explanation, it did not really fit the facts of the case. The marks were too high up the girder to have been made by a carriage simply toppling sideways off the rails. In any case, Bouch's theory was effectively demolished by Drummond's authoritative evidence to the Inquiry. Drummond was quite convinced that the carriages, in their headlong dive to the bottom of the river, had never left the track. He had observed in his inspection of the carriages that 'All the vehicles had their axles bent in one direction, which to my mind points clearly

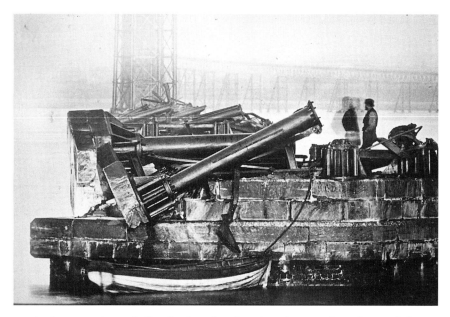

A photograph made for the Inquiry showing the remains of one of the cast-iron columns lying on its foundation. *Roland Paxton*

to the fact that the train had not been off the rails previous to the accident to the Bridge, but remained on the rails until it reached the water.'[133] In any case, acceptance of Bouch's theory would not and did not absolve him of moral responsibility, in that he had shown himself by his own admission to be the designer of a bridge which would fall down if struck hard enough by a light wooden carriage.[134]

In recent years, the idea that the train brought down the bridge has been given a new lease of life by the arguments of the late Mr William Dow, a physicist who had made a special study of the bridge and its fall. Dow accepted the view that the bridge collapsed because the last two carriages came off the rails, caught on the girders, and wrenched the bridge apart. At the heart of this explanation lies the so-called 'kink in the rails', a distortion of the line as it entered the high girders, itself the result, according to Dow, of the accident in 1877, when, in the course of construction, two of the high girders had been blown off the top of their columns into the river. One of these girders had been written off, but the other had been salvaged, repaired and re-used. In Dow's opinion, the girder had been weakened by its fall, had distorted in use, and since the rails were attached to wooden supports running the length of the girders, this distortion had resulted in the kink in the rails. The existence of this kink was well known to railwaymen, and had been brought to light in the course of the preliminary enquiries carried out by Thornton. It had not, however, been deemed to be sufficiently important to figure in the evidence at the inquiry.[135]

The plausibility of this theory does not depend, of course, on establishing a link with the 1877 accident. Whatever may have caused it there is no doubt that the kink did exist. The important question is therefore whether the kink derailed the train, and on that question there is no conclusive evidence. All the railway experts questioned about it at the time dismissed the kink as insignificant – a minor deviation which had had no effect on the running of the trains hitherto. On the other hand, the theory does square with some other evidence, not all of which came before the Inquiry. There was the assertion by the stationmaster at Newport, for instance, that he has seen, lying on the beach, a length of wooden planking from the floor of the bridge showing clear marks of the wheels of the train, suggesting that derailment had preceded the bridge's collapse. Incredibly he failed to secure this vital piece of wood, which was allowed to float away on the tide. There is also the undoubted fact that the coupling joining the second class carriage to the one in front was found to be broken, suggesting that it had been wrenched apart by some considerable force, such as might have been applied if the carriage had caught on the girders. There are the marks on the east side of the girders which Bouch had relied on to support his own theory. At the very least they suggest that train came into contact with the girders at some point, even if it cannot be proved that such contact occurred before the bridge actually fell.[136]

More recently Bouch's and Dow's explanation of the fall was taken up by Charles McKean, in his study of the rivalry between North British and Caledonian railways – *Battle for the North* – published in 2006. His description of the last moments of the passengers, train and bridge is dramatic:

> Barely a minute after leaving Barclay's cabin on the south shore, passengers on the train had probably felt an unusual jolt or bounce – a very sharp one in the case of the second-class carriage at the rear of the train – and then perhaps a dragging motion accompanied by the squealing of wheels against rails. The second-class carriage came to an abrupt halt, smacking into a girder tie-bar, and was immediately annihilated by the

heavier guard's van behind, which mounted up over it, crushing David Jobson and his companions to death. The force caused the cast iron columns below to fracture, and the bridge began to topple downstream into the foam.[137]

Unfortunately there is no real evidence to support this colourful account of the last seconds of the ill-fated train. While it is true that the second-class carriage was badly damaged, the damage was all on the side facing west, while it should have been on the side facing east. David Jobson's body was one of those recovered, but none of the recovered bodies showed the kind of injuries which would have resulted from the crushing force described by McKean.[138] Moreover, what this explanation does not fully take into account is the evidence of eyewitnesses as to the force of the wind at the time of the fall. Virtually every account links the collapse of the bridge with an enormously powerful gust of wind, a gust which forced all observers who were not indoors at the time to turn their backs on the wind or take shelter from it, at exactly the moment at which the bridge fell. Virtually every explanation of the collapse does likewise. In the edition which came out shortly after the disaster, the *Scotsman* reported that once the train had reached the mid-point of the high girders, 'at that moment a gust of wind more violent than any that had preceded it was experienced, and simultaneously the spectators noticed three separate streams of fire descend from the bridge elevation and disappear in the water, total darkness falling.'[139] The deck-watch on the *Mars* had been forced to turn his back on the bridge by the force of the wind. It is surely taking coincidence too far to suggest that the train was derailed by the kink at exactly the same instant as it was caught by a gust of wind.

Then there was the remarkably frank admission of Albert Grothe in the course of the Inquiry that despite all the assurances he had frequently given to Dundee audiences as to the ability of the bridge to withstand the force of any wind, however powerful, nevertheless he was now quite convinced that the bridge had simply blown down. James Brunlees, an engineer who, along with John Cochrane, had been brought in by the North British after the fall to carry out an investigation on the company's behalf, also supported this view in terms which remind us of the accounts of W.B. Thomson of the night the bridge came down. 'It appears to me,' Brunlees reported to his employers, that the immediate cause was an excessive wind force acting partly upwards on the floor of the bridge and horizontally on the piers, and girders and train. An undue stress was thus thrown on the three eastern columns of the piers tending to rupture the bracing between them and those on the western side, and from the position in which the wrecked train was found I believe no. 5 of the fallen piers was the one which succumbed to the undue strain thrown on it and fell, dragging after it the whole of the large spans.[140]

It is of course the central tragic fact of this whole story that the bridge collapsed as the train was passing over the navigation spans, and it is not surprising that a good many explanations of the fall link those two facts together. According to one contemporary account, so long as nothing was on the line,

the westerly wind passed freely through the latticing . . . and thus the slender structure remained almost unshaken by the fiercest wind strokes, but the moment that the train entered upon this portion of the bridge the conditions of the conflict were entirely altered. Not only did the quickly rolling body weaken the resisting power of the bridge by adding the sum of the vibration to that caused by the impact of the wind but, fatally as it happened, it presented also a solid body, upon which the strength of the wind could be exercised. This, it may almost be concluded, was the cause of the lamentable oc-currence.[141]

One of the most interesting contributions in recent years to the debate on the reasons for the bridge failure has come from Dr David Smith, a lecturer in civil engineering, who has argued strongly in favour of the view that the bridge simply blew down. Smith noted that of the main components of the bridge, both the girders and the founda-tions were essentially sound. Many of the 72 undamaged girders were retained in the structure of the new bridge and have lasted perfectly well for more than a century, while the foundations also have withstood the ravages of weather and water. It was the braced cast-iron columns which failed. He noted also that the columns and braces were defec-tive to some extent – the cast iron of the columns was not of the first quality, some of the wrought-iron bracings were imperfect, and some of the lugs to which the bracings were attached were unsound.

That said, he found that there was no evidence to suggest that 'either the columns or the bracings fell severely short of the strength they would have had if perfect', and having scrutinised the results of tests on both bracings and columns carried out after the fall, concluded that 'none of these figures justifies severe strictures on the quality or consistency of workmanship.'

'Calculations made after the disaster,' went on Smith,

> showed that a wind pressure of 1675 Newtons per square metre [34.99 lbs per square foot] would have been sufficient to rupture the weakest bracing, even assuming that 20 per cent to 25 per cent of the wind force was taken by the bending stiffness of the cast iron columns, and assuming the leeward girder to take 50 per cent of this pressure. It is difficult to see how the columns could take so large a pressure with all the bracings intact. If the share taken by the columns is neglected, the pressure to break the weakest bracing becomes at most 1340 Newtons per square metre [27.9 lbs per square foot].

Further calculations showed a high probability that this pressure of wind would be exceeded in the Dundee area at least once in every 50 years. From these two sets of figures Smith concluded, 'there is no reason to doubt that an extreme gale could have ruptured the weakest bracing. Once the weakest was ruptured the bracing on the opposite pier would be subjected to a force greater than the strength of the strongest bracing', and the collapse of the bridge would be the inevitable result. In short, Smith fully endorsed the findings of the first report of the Court of Inquiry, that 'the fall of the bridge was occasioned by the insufficiency of the cross bracing and its fastenings to sustain the force of the gale.'

Dr Smith's conclusions were given further support by a computer analysis of the bridge design carried out by Tom Martin and Professor Iain Macleod of Strathclyde University. According to their calculations, and using data supplied to the original Court of Inquiry, at a wind force of 10-11 on the Beaufort scale, simultaneous toppling and bracing failure were to be expected, with bracing failure the more likely outcome. This failure would very likely have occurred even without the additional wind resistance provided by the train. An interesting feature of their analysis was that the maximum wind bracing load was found to be part-way up the columns, rather than, as might have been expected, at the base. This conforms to an extent with what actually happened, where some of the columns fractured several feet from the bottom end.[142]

The consensus among many modern commentators is therefore that given the design of the bridge, the cross-bracing of the cast-iron columns was bound to fail if subjected to a force of wind equal to or greater than the gale which attacked it on 28 December, 1879. To that extent, their calculations, experiments and simulations have gone a long way to reinforce the principal conclusion of the Inquiry. It is important to stress, however, that it was not the tie bars themselves, but rather the lugs on the columns to which the tie bars were attached, which actually failed. John Cochrane, in his evidence to the Inquiry, confirmed that 'in the cases I have seen, I do not think I found any tie bars broken at all, practically it is the lugs that have gone.' Yet William Pole and Allan D. Stewart, in their technical report to Bouch in February 1880, had calculated that these lugs should have been capable of withstanding a load of 63 tons, and therefore a wind pressure well in excess of that

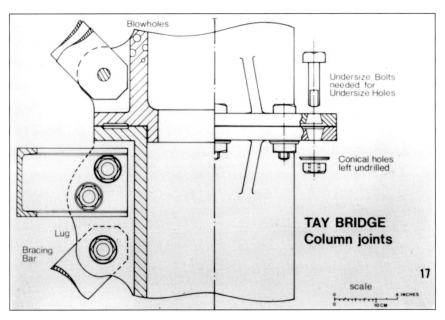

Diagram of a column joint, showing the attachment points of the cross braces. *Victor Bignell*

exerted by the great gale. Even more mysteriously, as we have seen, the evidence of tests carried out by Mr Kirkcaldy and reported to the Inquiry, revealed that the lugs he had tested had broken at very much less than 63 tons – some of them at less than one third of that figure. Pole, when questioned by the Court, accepted the test results, but was quite unable to explain them. 'My statement,' he told the Inquiry,

> simply amounted to this: that an engineer designing these lugs might on the ordinary rules expect them to bear 63 tons, with an average quality of iron. I know perfectly well that they have broken at Mr Kirkaldy's with less. I do not pretend here to explain why. Whether they have been damaged or not, I do not know, and I have no means of knowing. But the inference from that . . . is that the tie would break with a wind pressure of about 40 lbs.

Of course it is possible that Pole suspected that the low strength of the tie assembly was due to the conical seating for the bolt on the lug, but did not say so in order to protect Bouch. Pole was not the only witness before the Inquiry to be baffled by the test results. Edgar Gilkes, with much more experience of iron casting than Pole, confessed that the results

> puzzle me a good deal. They do not agree with the tensile strains we get from other parts of the same metal; that is to say the other parts of the same column, and I do not see any good reason for the difference unless it be that those lugs had undergone a severe straining before, and were not equal to what might have been expected from them afterward.

From this is would appear that Gilkes did not understand the amplification of the stress which would occur with conical seating of the lugs, and his suggestion that the metal was weaker in the lugs is not supported by any evidence. It is tempting, of course, to explain the failure of the lugs, as many previous commentators have done, in terms of poor workmanship at the Wormit Foundry. There is no real evidence for this either. While there might be the suspicion that the practice of 'burning on' the lugs accounted for their weakness, managers and workmen from the foundry had stated again and again that no columns with burned-on lugs had been incorporated in the structure of the bridge. While it is possible that they were lying to save their own reputations, no less a person than Henry Law, the Board of Trade's special investigator, conceded that in his examination of the broken parts of the bridge he had found no lugs that had been burned on. As we have seen, Yolland and Barlow attributed the great difference in strength between the metal of the columns and that of the lugs to the 'nature of the fastenings, which caused the stress to be brought on the edges or outer sides of the lugs, instead of acting fairly upon them.'

There remains one other explanation for the failure of the lugs which has attracted attention in recent years – the phenomenon of metal fatigue – a phenomenon unknown to engineers of Bouch's day, but suggested to the author by Mr William Dow some years ago.[143] More recently the issue of metal fatigue in the iron castings has been addressed in some detail by Dr Peter Lewis of the Open University, and his colleague Ken Reynolds, a forensic metallurgist.[144] Like Dow, they focus their attention on the 'kink' or, as they put it 'a slight misalignment of the track'. Trains passing over this kink, they argue, induced lateral oscillations in the high girders section of the bridge. Over time, as the joints holding the bridge together became progressively loosened, these oscillations became more pronounced, resulting in fatigue cracks appearing in the cast-iron lugs, until finally the lugs gave way and the result was a catastrophic disaster. While they accept that wind loads contributed to the collapse, their argument is that the bridge was already seriously defective before that event.[145]

To support their theory, they revisited the evidence produced at the Inquiry, and paid particular attention to the photographic evidence, especially that relating to the cast-iron lugs whose failure lay at the heart of the disaster. 'Close inspection of the fractures showed that they were not drilled out to give a parallel bearing surface for the bolts. On the contrary, the holes were cast as one with the lug and columns, and given a taper. This,' they assert, 'was a serious design defect, because it produced a severe stress concentration . . . when the bolt was stressed during straining of the bracing bars. The effect must have been to raise the stress at the outer edge of the hole by well over three times the nominal applied stress.' They also noted Henry Law's testimony to the Inquiry, in which he had pointed out that the bolts used to attach the tie bars to the lugs were too thin – only one and an eighth inches in diameter to fit the narrowest part of the tapered hole of one inch and a quarter. 'The bolts were therefore a very loose fit, inducing another stress-raising factor into the equation.' According to John Rapley, Bouch had agreed to Grothe's suggestion to use thinner bolts as a cost-saving measure.[146] If so, it was to prove a very costly mistake.

Even before the actual collapse of the bridge, there was evidence from men working on the bridge of severe vibration when a train passed over, both lateral oscillation and vertical movement – sufficient to cause water in a bucket to overflow the rim. And then there was the testimony of the unhappy Mr Noble, who had noticed the chattering in the structure, and had, as he thought, cured the problem by forcing metal shims into the loose joints. His evidence to the Court was dramatic:

> – Did you discover whether any of the ironwork of the bridge was getting unstable or loose?
> – In taking those soundings I spoke of, I noticed or heard a chattering of the bars.
> – Tell me what it was you found to be wrong with the bars on your examination of them.
> – I do not know whether I can explain it to you. I found that the cotters in coming together had got a little loose – there was not a sufficient width to get a good grip, and they had got a little loose.

It should be explained at this point that joints in the form of gibs and cotters were used only, in the structure of the Tay Bridge, to secure the lower end of the diagonal ties to the cast-iron lugs on the columns. They had a particular purpose – to enable tensioning of the tie bars on fitment by knocking the cotters together, this tensioning serving to stabilise the towers. By forcing pieces of iron bar into these joints, Noble had jammed the joints into a fixed state, bearing little or no strain from the tie bars. It was reckoned that Noble may have doctored as many as a hundred and fifty joints in this way.

Lewis and Reynolds conclude from this survey of the evidence that the bridge was already in a poor state even before the fateful night. Poor design, especially in the form of the conical holes in the lugs, poor maintenance, dangerously so, had resulted in a progressive loosening of the joints, and with it the destabilisation of the cast-iron towers. The action of passing trains, the regular battering of the malformed rail, induced metal fatigue in the lugs which then broke. In their view, while conceding that the force of the wind may have been a contributory factor, it was no more than that, the eventual disastrous outcome being well-nigh inevitable.

And what of the wind? We have seen how research published in 1993 by Tom Martin and Iain McLeod had come to a very different conclusion. In their view the action of the wind, and the failure at the design stage to build in a sufficient allowance for wind pressure, were the overriding factors in explaining the collapse of the bridge. If Lewis and Reynolds are adherents of the 'train brought down the bridge' thesis, then Martin and McLeod represent the view that the bridge simply blew down, taking with it the train. In 1995, and again in 2004, they have returned to this issue making use of the latest research methods, and arriving at much the same basic result.[147] We have to ask the question, wherein lie the very fundamental differences between Lewis and Reynolds on the one hand and Martin and McLeod on the other, to explain this very different set of conclusions?

We need to focus on two issues in particular – the pressure of the wind on the night in question, and the evidence for metal fatigue in the cast-iron lugs.

On the issue of wind pressure, Lewis and Reynolds have gone back to the testimony presented to the Inquiry, and in particular the opinion of one expert witness, Benjamin Baker, later to be one of the designers of the Forth Bridge. Experts had calculated that a pressure of around 35 pounds per square foot would be required to topple the high girders, but Baker's conclusion, after making a detailed survey of damage to walls and buildings in the vicinity, was that wind pressure on the night could not have been more than 15 pounds psf – far less than the predicted toppling pressure.

There were indeed no accurate scientific instruments present in Dundee at the time of the fall to measure the pressure of the wind, so the Inquiry had to rely on the views of unofficial observers, and these observers were largely agreed on a wind pressure of between 10 and 11 on the Beaufort scale. Martin and McLeod's calculations are based on a wind force of this order, which they present as between 28 and 36 pounds per square foot. This pressure of wind, they conclude, would have been sufficient to bring about an uplift in the base of the outer column on the windward (west) side of the bridge. The main effect of this uplift was to increase significantly the tensile load in the diagonal bracing members, leading to their failure. To quote from their 1995 article:

> On the basis of these observations a scenario for the collapse is as follows. When the train reached the high girders there was a particular strong gust. The presence of the train increased the overturning effect marginally, and the bolts in the windward columns came into tension. Because they were intended for location purposes rather than to take tension, they were not fully anchored into the masonry of the pier. The column bases started to lift off taking two courses of masonry with them. This had the beneficial effect of reducing the loads in the baseplate bolts, but caused a significant increase [of tension] in the diagonal bracing members, causing them to fail. These members first failed not at the bottom level [of the towers] but at a level above that. This triggered a toppling collapse with rotation tending to be at level 1. During the process of toppling there was a kickback to windward on the remains of the piers below level 1.

This graphic account of the sequence of events has the merit of conforming closely to the evidence presented to the Inquiry, both verbal and photographic. As we know, however, a key element in the failure of the bridge was the breakage of the cast-iron lugs – explained by Lewis and Reynolds as due to metal fatigue. Is it possible to reconcile the two rival interpretations by explaining the vulnerability of the bridge to severe wind pressure as due to the inherent weakness of the lugs caused by metal fatigue? The answer to that is 'probably not'. Martin and McLeod have no doubts that the disaster would have taken place even if the structure had been in perfect condition in accordance with the specification. The fundamental flaws in the design for the bridge were the failure to make adequate allowance for wind pressure, and the inadequate specification for the tie assemblics, or, as they put it in their 2004 paper, the applied wind load was much greater than the design wind load, and the actual strength of the ties was significantly less than the design strength of the ties, both with respect to the lug failure, and the failure of the tie itself.

Nor do they accept the case for the effects of dynamic motion and the onset of metal fatigue as presented by Lewis and Reynolds.

Drawing on the results of modern research into the failure of cast-iron castings due to metal fatigue, they conclude that the repeated stresses experienced by the component parts of the bridge over its lifetime would have been insufficient to cause fatigue. Nor do they accept the argument advanced by Lewis in his full-length book on the subject, that the fact that the collapse affected the high girders only was due to the absence of lateral girders, tying together the towers supporting the high girders.[148] Once again we are presented with the conclusion that the fundamental errors were to make inadequate allowance for wind pressure, and in the lug specification. All other explanations are mere footnotes to these facts.

THE QUESTION OF BLAME

It is one thing to arrive at conclusions as to the causes of the bridge failure, but it is, or may be, quite another to assign blame. Rothery's separate report, as we have seen, did both, and laid the blame for deficiencies of design, construction and maintenance mostly, though not entirely, as Bouch's door. Even Smith, who was sympathetic to Bouch and criticised Rothery for the extravagance of his attack on the bridge's designer, accepted that the reason for the collapse of the bridge was that Bouch did not make any specific allowance for wind force in his calculations. It remains open to question how far Bouch should be blamed for this, and whether others besides him should shoulder at least some of the moral responsibility for the disaster.

In the first place it is not strictly true that no allowance for wind pressure was made in the bridge's design. It is clear from the report of William Pole and Allan D. Stewart, submitted to Bouch on 25 February 1880, that Stewart had indeed made some allowance for wind pressure on his own initiative, though the allowance he made of only 20 lbs per square foot was clearly insufficient.[149]

At the Inquiry Bouch seemed curiously unaware of this fact. More to the point, there is clear evidence that in October 1869, when the bridge was still at the design stage, Bouch had made a written enquiry to the Board of Trade, asking what allowance should be made for wind pressure on lattice girders of up to 200 feet in length. (This was of course before the decision was made to increase the length of most of the girders to 245 feet.) Irony of ironies, his query was dealt with by none other than Colonel Yolland, who blandly informed him that 'we do not take the force of the wind into account when open lattice girders are used for spans not exceeding 200 feet'. No wonder that Yolland was unwilling to put his name to Rothery's attack on Bouch. Moreover, at the time when Bouch was obliged to redesign the bridge to take account of the new information about the nature of the river bed, he was also in the process of designing the Forth bridge, whose spans were to be a massive 1,600 feet long. Bouch took the precaution of consulting five of his most eminent colleagues in the profession (one of whom was W.H. Barlow, the third member of the Court of Inquiry) about the correct allowance for wind pressure, and it was they who then consulted Sir George Airy, the Astronomer Royal. The latter's recommendation of 10 lbs per square foot was used by Bouch to check the design of the Tay Bridge.[150]

It is true, as the Inquiry itself was told, that in France the usual allowance was 55 lbs, and in the United States, 50 lbs, but that information does not seem to have been widely known in Britain. It is difficult therefore to accept Rothery's view that Bouch should bear all the blame for a failure in design when, by all accounts, he had taken careful steps to acquire the latest information on the subject from the very experts who were later to sit in judgment on him.

Not that even Rothery assigned all blame exclusively to Bouch, and the Inquiry had revealed failures to fulfil their responsibilities on the part of almost everyone called before it who had had a role in its construction. The contractors, Hopkins Gilkes, and their representative as overall manager of the project, Albert Grothe, were criticised for their failure to construct the bridge to the necessary standards. Lesser figures, like Camphuis and Ferguson, were shown to be incompetent, and even honest Henry Noble, striving to do more than he was asked or qualified to do, had seriously failed to recognise his own limitations.

Yet should the real responsibility lie, not with these lesser men, but with their employers? Should not the North British, and its directors and shareholders, shoulder their share of the blame? Evidently the *Scotsman* thought so, and on the morning after the publication of Rothery's report weighed in with an attack on the Company for failing to exercise adequate supervision of the bridge's construction:

> There was evidently a degree of carelessness in the matter of supervising the bridge which was culpable and even scandalous. Sir Thomas Bouch may be to blame for not having looked

after Henry Noble; but ought not someone to have seen that Sir Thomas Bouch attended to his duty? Can the railway company be freed from blame? It is very difficult to do so . . . it is clearly the company and the company alone that must be held answerable to the public for whatever carelessness there was in the supervision and maintenance of the bridge.[151]

If it had chosen, though it did not, the *Scotsman* might have found other reasons to blame the company. It was the North British which had employed Bouch in the first instance – a man who had made his reputation as a designer of railway lines which were, like the St Andrews line, notable for their lightness and cheapness. He had also, by the time he came to design the Tay Bridge, acquired something of a reputation for unreliability. The company secretary of the small Leven line, of which Bouch was the designer, had endless trouble with him for failing to produce plans, to inspect completed sections of the line and to attend important meetings. In one of his plans, the measurements of every field were incorrect, and it had to be returned. 'Mr Bouch's want of attention to our present interests,' complained the harassed secretary, 'is a matter beyond our comprehension.' Similar problems were encountered by the promoters of the Crieff line, who also made the mistake of employing Bouch. While it is possible that the directors of the North British knew nothing of these problems, they should have done. When the company formed to extend the Leven railway along the Fife coast heard of the problems which had arisen with the Leven line, they decided to dispense with Bouch's services. It is perhaps worth noting also that Bouch's plans for Dundee's tramway system came in for severe criticism from the leading consulting engineers of the day.[152]

All along (except when it came to lavish self-congratulatory lunches) the North British had sought cheapness as the expense of durability. They had refused to fund the bridge itself, and passed that responsibility to the local men of the Undertaking; they had opted for a narrow and insubstantial single-line bridge, in place of a sturdier double line, solely on grounds of cost, and in the face of a good deal of local criticism. It is with a certain amount of grim satisfaction one notes that in the end it cost the North British something of the order of £1 million to bridge the Tay estuary.

And then again, the Inquiry, in casting counsel for the Board of Trade in the role of inquisitor, had pre-empted the question of the

Board's own responsibility. There was not just the matter of Yolland's advice to Bouch, but there was also the whole question of the Board's inspection and approval of the bridge in 1878. At a meeting of the Institution of Engineers and Shipbuilders in Scotland held in Glasgow early in 1880, the speaker, St John Vincent Day, exclaimed:

> I fail, in view of what I have seen for myself of the character of the structure, to comprehend how Major General Hutchinson could report that 'the iron work has been well put together in the columns and the girders'? Did he ascertain the depth and variation in depth of the holding down bolts? If so, his report is, to say the least, incorrect, for it has been abundantly shown how unfit was the structure of the columns for the functions imposed on them.[153]

The unfortunate Hutchinson had indeed been called to give evidence at the Inquiry, where he was forced to concede that his inspection had been superficial, and that he had not tested the bridge for the effects of wind pressure. In a separate report to the Secretary to the Board of Trade, Hutchinson insisted that he had found nothing wrong with the bridge during the three days of his inspection, and reminded the Board that at the time he had stipulated a speed limit of 25 m.p.h. It was not his fault if drivers ignored this restriction. On the matter of wind pressure he claimed that 'I was anxious to see how the lateral stiffness of the piers might be affected by the action of a high wind upon the side of a train in motion over the bridge. This I had intended to get if possible an opportunity of doing before the traffic commenced running, but I was laid aside by a serious illness shortly after the inspection and before my recovery the bridge had been opened to traffic.'[154] To fall ill was hardly Hutchinson's fault, but there had been nothing to stop Yolland sending a replacement inspector, which he had failed to do.

Not surprisingly, the failure of the bridge so soon after it had been passed as sound by the Board of Trade aroused considerable public concern. In his report Henry Rothery had defended the Board's position, and in the House of Commons debate on the fall of the bridge, President of the Board Joseph Chamberlain felt obliged to defend his Inspectorate on grounds of general principle. Hutchinson, he argued, 'could not be held responsible for any defects in the Tay Bridge which

114

were not discoverable in such an inspection which he was empowered to make . . . still less for defects which did not exist until after the inspection.' Moreover, Chamberlain insisted,

> the duty of an inspecting officer, so far as regards design, is to see that the construction is not such as to transgress those rules and precautions which practice and experience had proved to be necessary for safety. If he were to go beyond this, or if he were to make himself responsible for every novel design, and if he were to attempt to introduce new rules and practices not accepted by the profession, he would be removing from the civil engineer and taking upon himself a responsibility not committed to him by Parliament.[155]

Plausible perhaps, but not altogether convincing.

And yet, and yet. Even if it is accepted that others – both individuals and organisations – should share the blame with Bouch, it remains true that he was both legally and morally responsible for the failings of his design. It has been argued that in the matter of the underestimate of the allowance for wind pressure, for example, Bouch had taken reasonable precautions to enquire of the experts how much allowance should be made. It is difficult, however, to absolve him of all blame in the matter of those wretched cast-iron lugs. The Report of the Inquiry stated bluntly that

> it was in casting the holes through which the bolts, which held the ends of the struts and tie bars, passed, that the greatest mistake was made. These holes were cast in the lugs, and were already made, when they issued from the mould. We were told, however, that it is almost impossible to prevent the workers from casting the holes conical, as the cores can then be more readily removed, and accordingly we find that the holes in the lugs were for the most part, if not entirely, cast conical. The result was that the bolts, instead of having a plain surface to rest upon, as they would have had if the holes had been drilled or made cylindrical by riming, or drilling, bore only on one edge, and when a strain came upon them, they would of course give, until they got a bearing upon the sides of the holes.

In a very damaging exchange with Rothery, Bouch was forced to concede that the holes should indeed have been cylindrical, and that the bolts should have been wide enough in diameter to fill the holes. As it was, not only were the holes both conical and irregular in shape, but the bolts were appreciably thinner that the holes.

> The effect of these three things, namely the giving of the bolts so as to get a bearing on the sides of the holes, the irregularity of the holes in shape and position, and the holes being larger than the bolts, was to give a certain amount of play to the ends of the ties and struts; so that it was found, under Mr Kirkaldy's tests, that when the force was applied in the same direction as when in position on the columns, and by a steady pull without any shock, the lug was able to bear only one third of the pressure, which it should have done according to the amount of its sectional area.[156]

As we noted, one of Bouch's previous and supremely successful bridge designs had been the Belah Viaduct. So far from collapsing, the Belah survived for many years of successful service, and fell prey in the end not to metal fatigue or to the pressure of wind, but to the axe wielded by Dr Beeching in the 1960s. It too was constructed of cast-iron columns, and was very much taller than the Tay Bridge. But it differed from the Tay Bridge in three vital respects. First, its girders were much shorter, and their supports much closer together; second, the 'legs' of its supporting towers were much wider apart at the foot than they were at the top – what engineers call 'batter'; and third, its tie bars were not connected to the columns by cast-iron lugs at all – but by hoops of wrought iron which encircled the columns. At the Inquiry, Bouch was asked by Barlow why he had deviated from the method for dealing with the horizontal ties he had used so successfully at Belah, to which he replied 'They were so much more expensive, this was a saving of money.' But at what ultimate cost?

For this failure, it is difficult to absolve him from blame. The author has been in correspondence with a group of eminent civil engineers, and it is worth reproducing their views here *verbatim*:

> The critical faults in the design of the bridge were a) the underestimate of the wind forces on the structure, and b)

116

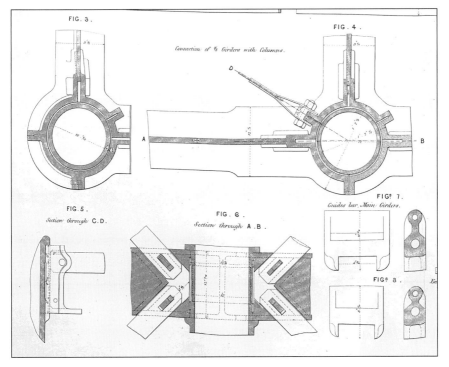

The ties used on the Belah Viaduct. *Roland Paxton*

the unsuitability of the tie assemblies. In relation to a) there were no written UK rules for wind loading when the Tay Bridge was designed. Therefore whether Bouch should be held negligent for using a low value for the wind force on the bridge is open to question. He knew it was an issue that should be considered but rather than play safe and use a high loading he used a low loading.

As to the design of the ties, whether or not there were written rules for connecting ties to columns (probably not), Bouch understood the fundamental principles of how to make such connections in a competent way, as evidenced from his design for the Belah Viaduct. He knew it was better to make a wrought-iron collar around the column and attach the ties to that. He knew that for best strength one should arrange that the bearing of a bolt on a support should be smooth and parallel to the line of the bolt – an elementary engineering principle. But he did not use these principles in the design of the connection to the column for the piers of the Tay Bridge. He compromised his own standards by allowing the bolts to bear unevenly on the cast-iron lugs because 'this was a saving of money'. He had staked his reputation on providing a low-cost bridge for his clients. Costs had already increased very significantly due to the early problems with the foundations, and he shaved down the redesign. He set the interests of his clients above that of the integrity of the bridge. One can say that his clients should not have pushed him in this direction, but that does not remove the responsibility from Bouch. It is a very difficult decision to make, but the code of ethics of professional engineering requires a consultant to refuse to continue with a client brief if the risk to the public becomes unacceptable. Bouch took a risk to save his reputation (for designing low-cost bridges) and put the interests of his client and himself above those of the public. That, in our view, made him guilty of negligence.[157]

EXIT SIR THOMAS BOUCH

It is hardly surprising that the Board, like everyone else involved, should disclaim responsibility, or that Chamberlain, like Rothery, should hold Bouch responsible. 'At the present moment,' Chamberlain assured Parliament, 'there is no one more deserving of pity than the civil engineer who designed and constructed the Tay Bridge and who also, as the law now stands, is held responsible for its defects.'[158] The question is, what did this all but universal condemnation have upon the unfortunate designer of the bridge, and how did he react to it?

The last day of the hearings before the Court of Inquiry was 8 May, a Saturday, and almost two months went by before its report was published. During those two months, Bouch worked on normally. Uppermost in his mind was the reconstruction of the Tay Bridge, which would require from him new plans for submission to Parliament, but there was also the great undertaking of the planned bridge over the Forth, not to mention the final piece of the east coast route – the bridge over the South Esk at Montrose. There seems to have been no doubt in his mind that he would continue to be responsible for all three projects.

Others were less confident. On 13 May, the North British board met in Edinburgh to consider the situation. One of the items for discussion was a letter from Adam Johnstone, chief solicitor for the North British Railway Company, suggesting that Bouch be got rid of, and the plans for the replacement be entrusted to a new engineer. At the time the board was not prepared to abandon Bouch, and George Wieland was instructed to send Johnstone a telegram affirming the board's position that Bouch must continue to be associated with the parliamentary plan for the reconstruction of the bridge.[159]

What Bouch now proposed was to improve the stability of the reconstructed bridge by reducing its height by 30 feet. The estimated cost of this plan, however, came to more than the sum allocated by the board for the reconstruction, and Bouch wrote to Johnstone on 17 May to suggest that the approach to Parliament should consist of a plan showing the bridge at its present height, but allowing for a reduction of up to 40 feet, once there was money to pay for it. Johnstone advised against this, and after more discussions between Bouch, Stirling, Falshaw and Walker, it was agreed to submit plans based on a reduction of 30 feet, but with the option of a further reduction to a total of 40 feet. Johnstone duly set to work on the draft parliamentary bill, but with little enthusiasm. More in touch with political opinion than most of his colleagues in the company, Johnstone had long been convinced that no proposal with which Bouch was associated would now be acceptable. Perhaps the senior members of the board understood this also, but were ashamed to be seen publicly to jettison Bouch. Privately they discussed the possibility of submitting the plans without his name on them. On 2 July the bill for the reconstruction of the Tay Bridge was introduced into the House of Lords, and allowed to pass standing orders unopposed, but with a warning to the company from Lord Riddesdale that it was likely to meet with opposition from both Houses in the following week. Three days later the news of the Court of Inquiry's two reports hit the headlines.[160]

The terms of these reports, especially Rothery's, must have been a severe blow to Bouch, but his first reaction was to stick to his guns. On the same morning, 5 July, he sent a telegram to Johnstone: 'Have seen report on bridge but am still going on completing my proof according to the deposited plans to enable you to complete your brief to counsel.' He then went round to see his solicitor, A.J. Dickson, whose sympathy for Bouch's feelings comes out strongly in a letter he wrote to Johnstone immediately after the meeting.

What an unmerciful report this is that has emanated from the Court of Inquiry. It seems too severe in every sense to be just

> . . . this report magnifies and rides to death (particularly the Wreck Commissioner's) every fault that can be picked and makes little allowance for the judgment of others and the possible imperfections, ignorance, or want of unbiased vision on the part of the Reporters themselves in a matter which could in all essential parts remain a mystery until the end of things.

Dickson was also angry on Bouch's behalf that Rothery had written his report in terms which suggested that his views were shared by Barlow and Yolland. Accordingly he wrote to Yolland, asking for clarification. 'Sir Thomas Bouch's position is under any circumstances sufficiently painful, and we are entitled to ask you to state in justice to him whether Mr Rothery was warranted in so representing your opinion as concurring with his in matters referred to you in this report.' To which Yolland and Barlow replied jointly that 'Mr Rothery was not warranted in representing our opinions as concurring with his own in matters not referred to in our report.'[161]

Bouch could be defended, but he could not be saved. In London Adam Johnstone, trying to prepare the ground for the discussion of the Tay Bridge Bill in Parliament, knew that it would face a hostile reception, and was convinced that Bouch would have to be dropped. He said as much in a telegram to the North British board, to which Wieland replied on their behalf that 'While we cannot entirely overlook Bouch, it is clear that independent engineers must be appointed for the Tay work.' John Stirling also took a pragmatic view, and in a letter to Johnstone told him that

> I should be very sorry to throw Bouch over altogether, but if it comes to a question of losing our bill we cannot help ourselves. This is my individual opinion. I was quite satisfied all along that although we might employ him to get our bill through parliament, yet to secure public confidence the plans, whatever they are, must have the sanction of a first class engineer, and I consider that Barlow, from his connection with the Tay Bridge Inquiry was the best man we could get.[162]

Even so, the North British found it difficult to bring themselves to tell Bouch to go. John Walker wrote to Johnstone on Bouch's behalf, suggesting, pointlessly, that while control over the bridge project must be put in other hands, Bouch's name might still be associated with it. Bouch himself was beginning to face up to the vulnerability of his position. Johnstone had written to him explaining the situation somewhat bluntly, and to this Bouch replied in a telegram that he 'had arranged to send up an assistant with bridge plan completed according to your parliamentary deposited plan, but after your letter suppose I had better wait reply.' That evening in the Commons both the promoters of the bill and Bouch in particular were subjected to a vitriolic attack from Mr Anderson, reputedly acting on behalf of the Caledonian Railway. 'The House has now to consider,' fumed Anderson,

> whether under these circumstances they ought to allow the very parties who are to blame to come to the house in the last month of the session and endeavour to rush through parliament a bill not for the construction of a new bridge under the supervision of new engineers, but a bill for the patching up of the miserable old structure. I myself have seen the plans and specifications, and they bear the name of Sir Thomas Bouch. Instead of coming to the house for a bill I think that some of the parties might rather be standing in a criminal dock to answer for their negligence.

Although the bill was granted a second reading, Bouch's position was by now untenable. Under authority from the North British board, Johnstone took action, appointing James Brunlees as the engineer for the reconstructed bridge, and telling Bouch what he had done, leaving him with no option but to resign. 'After the letter of yours dated the 13th,' Bouch duly responded, 'I must consider my position as engineer for the Tay Bridge to be terminated.'[163]

Time was running out both for the bridge and for Bouch himself. Parliament threw out the Tay Bridge Bill, and the Company, made aware that no scheme with Bouch's name attached to it had any chance of success, applied successfully to be allowed to withdraw their plans for a Forth Bridge. The great east coast dream which Bouch had harboured throughout his career was apparently over.

Bouch himself did not long survive this final disappointment. Although for a time he continued to work in his Edinburgh office on his few remaining projects, and he travelled to London at the end of July to defend the bill for the Edinburgh South Side and Suburban Railway, on the day after his return he fell seriously ill. On medical advice his wife took him to the Border town of Moffat to recuperate, but without success. Bouch died on 30 October, 1880, aged only fifty-eight, having survived the fall of his great bridge by only ten months.[164]

CHAPTER 8

FROM THE ASHES OF THE OLD

—=◦•◦=—

THE DECISION TO REBUILD

To rebuild the bridge across the Tay had been one of the first decisions taken by John Stirling after the initial disaster in 1879. It is
not difficult to see why. The enormous success of the first bridge in
bringing about an increase in the carriage of passengers and freight,
and therefore of income to the North British, was too great to be dis-
pensed with. To the loss of income caused by the destruction of the
bridge should be added the capital loss in share values. When trading
began on the Monday following the accident, shares in the company
opened at almost ten per cent below their previous value, representing
according to one account a loss in one day equivalent to the whole cost
of constructing the bridge, though it is true that within a year the value
of the shares had been restored. And of course the bridge itself had
gone – a huge capital asset which before it fell had become the property
of the North British, the company having agreed to take it over from
the shareholders in the Undertaking on payment of a premium of £30
per share in lieu of accrued interest. Then there was the capital value
of Taybridge Station and all its connecting lines, which would remain
worthless until such time as the bridge came to be rebuilt.[165]

The decision to rebuild must have met with the approval of the
majority of Dundonians, and not only those with business interests to
serve. The people of the city, not to mention the inhabitants of Fife,
had become accustomed in the few months of its operation to the great
convenience which the bridge had afforded them of easy access to the
opposite shore of the river, and they were unwilling to go back to the
inconvenience of the ferry. The loss of the bridge would have been felt
particularly in Newport, whose main water supply had been cut off
when the collapse of the bridge severed the pipe line, and where as a
consequence of the new rail connection with the northern shore a great
number of houses had been built for Dundee's prospering middle class.

Rather less enthusiastic about the rebuilding of the bridge, to be sure, were the tradesmen and Town Councillors of Perth. Resigned to the replacement of the bridge with a new but similar structure, they were extremely angry to learn of a move by the Town Council of Dundee to try to get the height of the bridge reduced to a mere 40 feet above the level of the water. All the old arguments and jealousies of the previous decade resurfaced, as the men of Perth accused 'these sapient and supreme gentlemen of Dundee' of seeking 'to decree the complete extinction of the Tay as a navigable river'. Perthshire newspapers painted extravagant pictures of the future of their town as a potential rival to Glasgow, if only they were allowed to develop the navigation of the river unhindered by the Tay Bridge. Sympathy for their plight came indeed from a correspondent in Glasgow, who described the people of Perth as

> the victims of a cruel set of circumstances. Perth, as the most ancient town on the Tay, possessing since the twelfth century the right to levy dues on the river, might be supposed to have a prescriptive right to all the advantages the river can give. Yet the rights of Perth are to be put on one side by the upstart Dundee, which never had a royal charter, and which was a howling wilderness when Perth was a Royal residence.

In the end the matter was resolved in exactly the same way as it had been resolved in 1870 – by cash. Under the 1870 arrangement, the Company had agreed to pay to the Perth Corporation an annual sum of £25 for every foot of reduction in height from the original 100 feet. This arrangement was now extended to cover further reductions in height, at the same rate per foot.[166]

As we have seen, once the report of the Court of Inquiry had been published, the North British had lost no time in filing a new application to Parliament for a bill to repair and restore the original bridge. This proposal was remitted to a Special Committee, which was given very specific instructions to report

> as to whether the Tay Bridge should be rebuilt in its present position, or whether there is any situation more suitable, having regard to the safety of the travelling public and the convenience of the locality. That their special attention be directed to the

124

interests of the navigation, and that the height of the bridge shall be so fixed as not injuriously to interfere with the river navigation. That they shall consider generally in what way any bridge that may be authorised should be constructed so as to secure its permanent safety.

This Committee came unanimously to the view that the application according to the plans submitted to Parliament should not be granted, but recommended nevertheless that the bridge should be reconstructed on its present site, with its spans over the navigational channel lowered from 88 to 77 feet.[167]

W.H. BARLOW

Faced with this outcome, the directors decided to call on the services of W.H. Barlow, one of the members of the Court of Inquiry and an engineer of the highest reputation, to advise them on how they should now proceed with reconstruction, on the basis of a double-line bridge. Barlow was determined to take no chances, and before he produced his report he carried out a number of investigations and experiments. The first step was to take a series of soundings along the line of the bridge to find out what had been the effect of the scouring action of the river, and then to take borings at 500 foot intervals on a line parallel to the centre line of the old bridge. What these investigations showed was that the construction of the old bridge had caused a deepening of the river, especially in the area where the ebb tide was strongest. The total area of the waterway occupied by the piers was equivalent to about one tenth of the total waterway of the river, and it was found that the effect of the scour was to restore to the river about the same area as was taken up by the piers. The result of the borings was to show that close to the shore on either side the river bed was of whinstone, and from the southern shore as far as pier no. 12 of the old bridge was sandstone. From the rock on both sides for about 900 feet towards the centre of the river there extended a strip of tough boulder clay, but the remainder of the river bed consisted of silty sand, in which there were beds of gravel of varying thickness.

Two experiments were now carried out to test the load-bearing capacity of the river bed. First, two of the piers of the old bridge were loaded with 1,500 tons of rails, producing a pressure of a little over 3.5

tons per square foot. One of these piers, situated in clean sand, sank a mere quarter of an inch, while the other, in micaceous sand, sank two inches. Next a trial cylinder was sunk to a depth of 20 feet in the area showing the worst silty sand, filled with concrete, and loaded to a gross weight of 7 tons per square foot. This produced a settlement of five and a quarter inches, but it then sank no further, even after the weights had been left in place for three-and-a-half months.

Barlow and his team now produced four separate designs and estimates for the construction of a double-line bridge. Only one of these was for an entirely new structure. The other three would all have involved keeping the old bridge intact, and either widening it on one or both sides, or constructing an additional single line bridge alongside, and bracing the two structures together. There were serious difficulties in all three schemes, despite the cost savings which would arise from making use of the original structure. The main problems had to do with the insecurity of the old foundations, which it was found had not been sunk deep enough to protect them from the effect of scour, and would require reinforcement. To do this was made more difficult by the fact that Grothe and his team had produced so many different forms of foundations – some single cylinders, some double, some elliptical, some on piles, and some partly square and partly round.

There were two other important considerations: first that the Board of Trade had by now specifically prohibited the use of supports consisting of cast iron braced with wrought-iron ties, and second that the standing parts of the old bridge were ideally placed to bring up men and materials to build the new one, provided the new one was built alongside the old. The plans which involved incorporating the structure of the old bridge with the new were therefore discarded; Barlow recommended to the directors that they build a new bridge, and his advice was accepted.[168]

In designing his replacement of the old Tay Bridge, Barlow was clearly going to take special care to avoid the mistakes of his predecessor. Thorough calculations were carried out to make allowance for the effects of wind pressure on the structure, and these calculations were based on a pressure of 56 lbs per square foot. Moreover, as Barlow's son explained to fellow members of the Institution of Civil Engineers in March 1888, his father had erred heavily on the side of caution, and 'in estimating the overturning effect produced by this force, the parapet and train were treated as presenting a plane surface of resistance; the girder as a surface one and a half times its actual area, and the octagonal side of the pier as a square surface; with these conditions the balance of effects was largely in favour of gravity.'[169]

In many ways, however, the design of the new bridge was similar to that of the old. 10,711 feet in length, with eighty-five piers, and sited 60 feet upstream from the old bridge, it followed much the same line across the estuary, the two centre lines running parallel for the whole of the straight central section of 8,396 feet. In outline, seen from the side, the two would have been hard to tell apart, were it not for the difference in height. The piers of the new bridge were placed exactly in line with the old ones, whose bases now formed the cutwaters for their new counterparts. Moreover, the lattice girders from the surviving spans of the old bridge were found to be perfectly suitable for re-use as the outward parapet girders of the new. All that was needed to provide the width necessary for a double-line bridge was to install two new girders between each pair of old ones.[170]

The overall similarity in the design of the two bridges conceals some important differences in both design and construction. At the southern end of the bridge, where branch lines were led off to the west across Fife and to the east towards Newport, the old arrangement had been for the branches to be carried by two separate viaducts, joining the bridge at some distance from the shore, and with the waters of the river clearly visible between them. In order to comply with the conditions laid down by the Parliamentary Committee in 1880, the branch lines to the new bridge joined it at a point much nearer to the shore, and were supported on brick arching wide enough to carry both of them. At the northern end, the great eastward curve of the rails of the new bridge was made gradually to approach the line of the original as it drew into Taybridge Station. Out in the middle of the river there were once again to be thirteen high girders over the navigable channel, but their height above high-water level was reduced from 88 to 77 feet.

No less important than these changes to the original design were substantial changes to the construction of the bridge, beginning with the foundations. These were now to be in the form of twin wrought-iron cylinders, 16½ feet in diameter, but widened out at the base to 23 feet, and filled with concrete and brickwork. One and a half feet above high-water level these were joined together with a horizontal member of concrete and brickwork seven feet deep, resting on cast-iron supports, and across the whole was fixed a strong wrought-iron frame, which was to provide the base for the wrought ironwork of the piers above. The frame itself was secured to the foundations with sixteen wrought-iron tie bolts, anchored to cast-iron plates set in concrete. Above these came the piers themselves, constructed neither of brickwork, as in the original Bouch design, nor of the now discredited cast-iron columns, but of plates of wrought iron riveted together. These piers took the forms of two hollow octagonal columns joined by a connecting arch, supporting the superstructure which, although it was to be constructed of the same kind of lattice girders as the original, was now to be supplied with a deck of corrugated steel, instead of wood.[171]

WILLIAM ARROL AND CO

The Parliamentary Bill for the construction of the new Tay Viaduct received the Royal Assent in July 1881, and by October the firm of William Arrol and Co. of Glasgow had been appointed as contractors. Arrol was one of the great bridge engineers of his day, and among his successes to date had been the iron bridges for the Glasgow, Hamilton and Bothwell Railway, including a large bridge carrying the rails at a considerable height over the Clyde near Bothwell. He was both methodical and innovative, and amongst other ingenious inventions he had designed a hydraulic riveting machine which was soon in general use in bridge and ship building. Arrol had originally been engaged by the North British to build Bouch's bridge over the Forth, and when that scheme was abandoned he was given the contract to reconstruct the bridge over the South Esk at Montrose. It was Arrol of course, who built the present bridge over the Forth.[172]

Arrol and Co. had intended to make a start on the replacement bridge at the end of 1880, but they were prevented from doing so by legal wrangles over the terms of the bill which, in its final form, had included a clause requiring the company to 'remove the ruins and debris of the old bridge and all obstructions interfering with the navigation caused by the old bridge, to the satisfaction of the Board of Trade.' The interpretation put upon this clause by the Board was that the process of clearing away the remains of the old bridge must precede any work on the new, and as the estimate for the new bridge had been based on the use of the old lines to carry men and materials out to the new bridge in the course of construction, as well as the re-use of girders from the low sections of the old bridge, the position adopted by the Board caused serious difficulties. The dispute was eventually resolved, but only after the loss of several months, with the result that work on the bridge did not begin until June 1882, and the first foundation was not laid until early in the following year.[173]

BUILDING THE NEW BRIDGE

Once started, however, the work under Arrol's expert supervision progressed smoothly and swiftly. The method of construction was similar to that used on the old bridge, but with some significant improvements, most notably in the design of the pontoons for sinking the foundation cylinders, and in the extensive use of steam-driven and hydraulic machinery in place of manual labour. As with the old bridge, the cylinders for the foundations were built on shore and floated out to their positions by pontoons. But Arrol's pontoons, unlike Gilkes', were fitted with four large cylindrical legs which could be raised or lowered by hydraulic power. With the legs standing firmly on the river bed, the

One of William Arrol's 'quadrupeds' – a pontoon fitted with hydraulic legs which could be lowered to rest on the river bed. The pontoon was also equipped with a steam shovel. *Dundee City Library*

Two of the buckets for the steam shovel, showing the triangular 'teeth'
which bit into the river bed. *Dundee City Library*

height of the pontoon itself could by adjusted up or down hydrauli-
cally. As a result, the pontoons were extremely steady, even in rough
weather, and the operation of sinking the cylinders could be carried out
with unusual accuracy. A visitor to the site described the operation of
these great pontoons or 'quadrupeds':

> Though the water was very rough, it made no impression
> on the vessel, for the simple reason that the hydraulic power
> on board had been applied, and the quadruped, unlike most
> quadrupeds, had lengthened its legs until the water was some 6
> feet below its bottom. It matters not how stormy the weather
> might be, operations can always be carried on on board.

These pontoons also carried a good deal of steam-powered equipment – steam engines for powering the excavating equipment and
concrete mixing machinery as well as steam cranes. It was therefore
possible to do more of the construction of the cylinders on site than
before – only the metal work was fabricated before the cylinders were
floated out to their final positions, and the construction of the brick

lining inside each cylinder was completed on board the pontoon. As before, the cylinders were fitted with a flange or internal ledge on which brickwork was built up before the whole was lowered into position on the river bed. The inside of the cylinder was excavated by steam digger, until it had been sunk to the required depth, and the whole was then filled with concrete.[174]

In December 1885 the site was visited by David Carr, a reporter for the *Pall Mall Gazette*, who recorded a graphic description of the scene:

> Clouds of steam and the noise of rattling chains fill the air as we leave the deck of the launch that has brought us from the shore and ascend, with the cautious steps of unpractical feet, the encircling staging of the huge caissons which, in a double line, are being sunk across the broad estuary of the Tay. Clambering over a mass of beams and planks, we reach the platform at the summit, and watch the steam excavators at their work as they hang suspended, like the drawn fangs of some mighty giant, over the gaping mouth of each iron cylinder. With a sudden movement they sink from sight and plunging downwards are lost in the sandy bottom of the river. The laboured snorting of the engine marks the tightened strain upon the chains which, by their upward action, close the sharp pointed blades, and bring to light a mass of stones and mud. As the load nears the surface and rises clear above the iron edge, the long arm of the crane, obedient to a touch, swings round, and sends the dripping gravel out into the turbid waters of the stream below. Slowly the massive column descends, and length is added upon length till it will sink no further, even when weighted with a load far greater than it will ever have to carry. This point once reached, the excavation ceases, and the hollow core is lined with brickwork and filled with a solid mass of concrete.[175]

In his evidence to Parliament in support of the bill to build a new bridge, W.H. Barlow had undertaken to test the foundation of every single pier with a weight equal to one third more than that produced by the weight of the structure added to the rolling load of the traffic on both set of rails. This undertaking was included in the bill, and faithfully

Many of the old girders were used in the new bridge. Arrol devised a tall pontoon with hydraulic jacks to transfer the girders from their original columns to the new supports. *St Andrews University, Valentine Collection*

adhered to. After each pair of cylinders had been filled with concrete, iron girders were placed across them, and loaded with weights until all subsidence ceased. A careful check on the process was kept by Major Marindin for the Board of Trade, who became a frequent visitor to the site.

Once the testing had been completed, the wrought-iron piers were built up on their bases. Each pier was in the form of a pair of octagonal hollow legs, joined at the top by an arch, and was initially built up and fitted together at the Arrol works in Glasgow, before being dismantled and transported to the site of the bridge. The same process was followed with the new girders, though these were reassembled on shore, as with the old bridge, and floated out to the piers in much the same way as before – on pontoons hauled out by steam tugs. Once in position they were lifted by hydraulic presses, and the plates of the piers progressively riveted in place beneath them. In the case of the old girders salvaged from the surviving sections of the old bridge, these were transferred across to the new ones on pontoons which once again were specially designed by Arrol for the purpose. The girders were supported on telescopic legs which could be raised or lowered to allow for the state of the tide. With the pontoon stationed underneath a girder, the rise of the tide was sufficient to raise it from its bed plate, from where it could be floated the 60 feet across to its new home.[176] It was a remarkable record that the entire process of floating out and lifting the girders was accomplished without either failure or accident.

After the initial delays caused by the dispute over the removal of the remains of the old bridge, work had begun in earnest in the early spring of 1882. In less than eighteen months substantial progress was reported in sinking the foundations of the piers, which by this stage were being constructed at the rate of one a week. Work was also far advanced on building the first three piers from the north end, for the construction of which huge coffer dams were being built, the first of them out of great logs 11 inches square, and between 24 and 40 feet long, to suit variations in the river bed. The caissons took the form of two concentric rings with a gap of two feet between them, the gap being filled with quantities of clay supplied by the Glencarse Pottery. By the end of September 1883, *The Times* reported, nineteen piers had been completed, and it was expected that the whole bridge would be finished by the late summer of 1885.[177]

The new high girders being hoisted into position. *Dundee City Library*

This was perhaps over-optimistic, and would have meant that the new bridge would have been completed in less than half the time taken to build the old. But the man from *The Times* was not alone in his admiration for the great skill and efficiency of Arrol and Co., and the effective use they were making of modern steam-powered machinery. 'A visitor to the works,' commented one such in February 1884,

> is very much impressed by the quiet, methodical manner in which the operations are being carried on. The large number of powerful and intricate machines employed in preparing the material for the structure turns out enormous quantities of work, which not long ago was done by manual labour, and is striking evidence of the advance made in recent years by mechanical engineering.[178]

By May of the same year, another visitor was able to report that

> all the foundations from pier 54 to pier 85 have been laid, and the cylinders are all more or less advanced. Pilasters have been put into the face of pier 86 (the easternmost column of the first brick arch) to make the old and new brickwork join better together. Piers 84 and 85, which carry the bowstring girder over the footway of the Esplanade [this was before the roadway on the Esplanade had been extended to its present length] have been finished, and a wooden staging has been erected for the building of the girders. The skew brick pillars which have been built in anticipation of the extension of the Esplanade are now in an advanced state. It is the intention of the contractors to erect the girders of the new bridge at the north end as soon as the piers are ready. Cast-iron connecting bases have been placed on the cylinders of two of the piers (54 and 55) which are now ready for the brickwork from which will spring the malleable iron superstructure. The piers are being systematically tested by the Board of Trade, and the results have proved eminently satisfactory to all concerned.[179]

By the beginning of January 1885, all but a handful of the pier foundations had been sunk, while the superstructure of all the piers on the south side as far as pier 13 was ready to receive their girders. At the

Demolition of one of the old brick columns. *Dundee City Library*

north end, all 43 foundations stretching from the northernmost of the high girders to the Esplanade had been laid. On 32 out of the 43 the superstructure was also complete, while 23 of them had also been fitted with their girders, ready for the rails. On the Dundee shore the bridge was by now joined to the brick viaduct carrying the rails into Taybridge Station, so that most of the work still to be done was on the water. By now the workforce had been increased from 200 to 630, and the work of construction was carried on by night as well as by day, through the use of powerful Lucigen electric floodlights.

Not only was the construction of the bridge proceeding at a much faster pace than had been the case with the first bridge, but the structure exhibited a welcome appearance of stability and solidity lacking in its predecessor. To an observer of the almost finished structure in the autumn of 1885 to overall effect was reassuring.

The increased basal area of the cylinders, and the breadth and solidity of the superstructure will give stability to the bridge and will no doubt inspire the public with confidence in its permanence. The girders, being doubled in number, have, as compared with the old Bridge, a much more substantial appearance, and the screens with which they are surmounted on

135

either side give a different aspect to the new Bridge and impart to the visitor when walking along the permanent way a feeling of security. In their design the Messrs Barlow have discarded all new or tentative methods in bridge architecture. They have evidently striven to model a strong and durable bridge, and to attain those qualities they have proceeded on well-known and fully recognised principles.[180]

Two Inspections

In June 1886 the directors of the North British decided on an inspection not only of the new Tay Bridge, but also of the great bridge over the estuary of the Forth, now under construction. Unlike previous such inspections, this was no carefree jaunt, but a hard day's work taken seriously by all those involved. 'Time was,' commented the *Advertiser* with a certain nostalgia,

> when such an inspection by the North British directorate implied for the most part a pleasant holiday. Ten years ago, to go no further back, one might count upon pleasant companionship and blithe talk, into which politics and commerce entered hardly at all, and a minimum of inspection, and an elegant dinner at the residence of one or other of the merchant princes of Dundee – shall we say the late Provost Cox of that busy manufacturing town? But many things have happened since then, and the directors of railway companies, in the interest of their shareholders, must now take things more seriously, and live laborious days, inspecting two concerns, either of which is enough at a time, and shun the wholesome delights of an early dinner . . . The inspection by the directors, it may be said, was no mere general look around. Practical men accompanied them, answering questions, and offering explanations. Not contented with what they had seen on the bridge, the directors, after a hurried luncheon at the offices on the Dundee shore, sailed round the piers, and were able to say generally that the work has made great progress since their last visit, and that the end is now within measurable distance.[181]

Testing the new bridge. *Dundee City Library*

On 16, 17, and 18 June 1887, the Board of Trade inspectors, (including amongst them our old friend Major General Hutchinson) came to Dundee to carry out their inspection. They ran eight coupled engines on each track, and tested for vibration and deflection of the structure – the effect was negligible. They took soundings in the river to measure the effect of scour on the foundations – they were wholly satisfied with the result. They spoke 'in very high terms of the substantial and skilful manner in which the bridge had been constructed', and sent a telegram to the Board in London to record their complete satisfaction with the structure. A mere three and a half hours later the first train to cross the bridge set off on its short journey carrying, as the *Advertiser* recorded, 'the Provost, Magistrates, and Town Council of Dundee, along with their lady friends, numbering in all 200, and it is to be hoped that the pleasure experienced by the passengers in that train will be the experience of all those who will cross the viaduct in all time coming.' On its return to Taybridge Station the train was met with a salute of 21 fog signals, before the passengers alighted to partake of cakes and wine in the station dining room. A mere two days later the bridge was opened for passenger traffic, and without further ceremony the first scheduled train left Dundee for Fife at 5.05 a.m. on Monday 20 June, 1887.[182]

It had taken five more years of construction work, and an aggregate expenditure for the two bridges of almost £1 million, but the North British now had their permanent bridge across the river Tay. Let William McGonagall have the last word, even if his knowledge of engineering was even less sure than his skill as a poet:

> Beautiful new railway bridge of the Silvery Tay,
> With your strong brick piers and buttresses in so grand array,
> And your thirteen central girders which seem to my eye,
> Strong enough all windy storms to defy.[183]

HOW MANY WERE LOST
IN THE DISASTER?

In the highly charged atmosphere in the hours immediately following the loss of the train, some wildly inaccurate estimates of the loss of life were current. According to the *Dundee Courier and Argus* of 30 December, 1879, first reports spoke of 200 victims, while Mr Walker, the manager of the North British Railway Company, dispatched a telegram stating that 'he deeply regretted to say that there were nearly 300 passengers, besides Company servants, on the train.'

At the same time Walker set in motion an inquiry to try to ascertain a more accurate figure. The procedure followed by this inquiry was to examine the record sheets kept by the collector of tickets at St Fort Station – the last stop before the bridge itself – since it was normal practice for tickets for Dundee to be physically collected at this station. Tickets for Broughty Ferry, Newport and any stations further to the north were examined, but then left with the passengers for collection at their final destination. Season tickets were similarly retained by their holders. According to this procedure, 75 tickets had either been collected from passengers, or inspected and returned, but to these should be added the number of children with no tickets, and several servants of the railway company – an estimated total of around 90.

The previous day, 29 December, the *Courier*'s sister paper, the *Evening Telegraph*, had published a list of named victims totalling only 24, and a list of tickets collected at St Fort totalling only 56. To this figure should be added, according to the report, a number of children with their parents, two third-class tickets from King's Cross held by two young ladies of about 18 years of age, five third-class tickets actually issued at St Fort and not included in the list, and about five passengers to Broughty Ferry. There was an unknown number of through passengers, and a few season-ticket holders.

By the afternoon of the next day, 30 December, the *Telegraph* reported that ticket collectors at St Fort were now convinced that the number of persons on the train, excluding infants and children travelling without tickets, could not have exceeded 75. This number was made up of 56 ticket holders whose tickets had been collected, 5 passengers to Newport, and 6 to Broughty Ferry. Added to this were two season-ticket holders, three guards, one mail guard, the driver and the fireman – 75 in total.

At the official Inquiry into the Disaster held initially in Dundee, similar figures were advanced. William Friend, the ticket collector at St Fort, stated that he collected tickets from the forepart of the train, altogether 56 tickets. There were two season ticket holders, and five or six for Broughty Ferry, who did not give up their tickets. Among the tickets were two halves. Altogether the tickets represented 57 or 58 persons, to whom should be added those who did not give up their tickets.

The porter at St Fort, who had helped Friend to collect tickets, confirmed to the Inquiry that the practice was to collect tickets only from passengers for Dundee – passengers going further retained their tickets. Four passengers in the second class were going to Newport, and so he did not take their tickets. (This may seem odd, in that Newport is *south* of the river. On weekdays, passengers to Newport from the south would normally change trains at Leuchars. But on the Sabbath they were obliged to continue across the bridge and take a local train or the ferry back to Fife. The ferry terminal was literally within a stone's throw of the station.)

Finally, Robert Morris, the stationmaster at St Fort, who had also taken part in the collection, reported that he had made up a list of all tickets collected. This list showed whether they were singles or returns, and where they were issued. The total number was 56, plus 2 half tickets. 'The persons who gave up their tickets and those who did not give up their tickets represented everybody in the train he saw.' Some support is given to this figure by the existence of a collage of tickets, claimed to be the tickets collected at St Fort, now on loan to the City Museum in Dundee from the family of stationmaster Morris. The collage contains 55 tickets, including two half tickets, and each of the tickets shows the name of the station at which the ticket was bought, and the destination. (The half tickets are literally one ticket, from Leuchars, cut in two – possibly the two children's tickets referred to in the Inquiry report.)

Scrutiny of the collage reveals that all of the tickets contained in it show Dundee as the final destination of the ticket holder, supporting the evidence of the St Fort staff that they collected tickets only from the Dundee-bound passengers. The absolute accuracy of the exhibit may be called into question, however, given that there is not an exact match between all the tickets in the collage, and the known embarkation points of the victims. For example, there are 7 tickets with the embarkation point Perth, but only two victims in the official death list can be traced back to Perth, and six passengers are known to have embarked at St Fort, but there is only one ticket from St Fort in the collage.

In his summing up, Chairman of the Inquiry Henry Rothery stated that there were 72 or 75 persons on the train, including the Company's servants. That is – 57 including two half tickets, 4 company's servants, 2 guards not on duty, 1 mail guard, 5 persons for Broughty Ferry, and 5 or 6 for Newport.

The figure of 75 has been widely accepted by subsequent commentators as the extent of the death-toll in the disaster. This was the number adopted by John Prebble in his seminal history of the event – *The High Girders* (1956). The same number, or one close to it, has been accepted by several subsequent writers on the subject, such as John Thomas in *The Tay Bridge Disaster – New Light on the 1879 Tragedy* (1972); Peter Lewis in *Beautiful Railway Bridge of the Silvery Tay* (2004); Charles McKean in *Battle for the North* (2006), though he chose 72; and most recently by Robin Lumley in *The Tay Bridge Disaster – the People's Story* (2013). Prebble did not spell out how he came by this information – *The High Girders* is not supplied with either footnote references or a bibliography – but in all probability it came from the two sources quoted above: the Dundee newspapers of the day, and the Report of the Board of Trade Inquiry.

And yet that is not at all the end of the story. Other evidence exists which offers a very different tally of the victims. From time to time both the *Telegraph* and the *Courier* published the actual names of victims, as distinct from the list of tickets. The latest of these, in the *Courier* for 1 January 1880, totalled only 56. The police list, held in the Police Museum in Dundee, records 60 names, though one of these (James Paton) was not actually a victim, and this figure is cited in Andre Gren, *The Bridge is Down* (2008), and the first edition of the present book. Most important of all, the National Register of Archives for Scotland lists 59 death certificates for victims of the disaster. It was this figure and this list of the names of victims which were adopted by the Tay Rail

141

The memorial to the victims erected by the Tay Bridge Disaster Memorial Trust in 2013.

Bridge Disaster Memorial Trust in 2013, as the tally of people, men, women and children, who were *known to have died* in the fall.

The question is – can these two figures be reconciled, or the wide difference between them be explained?

In the first place it should be understood that the two sets of figures were arrived at by quite different means. As is clear, the figure of 75 or thereabouts was derived solely from the list of tickets collected at St Fort station, or more accurately, the 56 tickets which were collected at St Fort plus the passengers and crew who either did not need tickets, or who retained them for the onward journey. The circumstances for carrying out an accurate count were hardly ideal. There have been suggestions that the bag into which the tickets were put already had some tickets from the previous train. A fierce gale was blowing, there was pressure to get the count over as quickly as possible, but was that sufficient to lead to such a wide discrepancy?

On the other hand the list of the 59 named victims was derived not from the count of tickets, but from the testimony of North British officials and the friends and relatives of the passengers. All but two of the named victims were local people, and it is a reasonable assumption that if there were any more victims, most of those would also have been

142

locals. Are we to understand that as many as 15 or 16 victims had no relatives, friends or business colleagues to report their disappearance?

Where then does this leave the question of the number of victims? The wording on the memorials to the victims erected in 2013 is specific – it names the 59 victims *who are known to have died* in the Disaster. There may have been more, but if so we do not know their names or how many there were. Until new and compelling evidence comes to light to add to this list, it must stand.

LIST OF KNOWN VICTIMS

Name	Age	Occupation	Address
Anderson, Joseph Low	21	compositor	13 South Ellen Street
Annan, Thomas Ross	20	iron turner	48 Princes Street
Bain, Archibald	26	farmer	Mains of Balgay
Bain, Jessie	22	sister of above	Mains of Balgay
Beynon, William Henry	39	photographer	Cheltenham
Brown, Elizabeth Hendry	14	tobacco spinner	28 Arbroath Road
Cheape, or Roger, Euphemia	51	domestic servant	99 High Street, Lochee
Crichton, James	22	ploughman	Mains of Fintry
Cruickshanks, Annie	54	domestic servant	Moray Place, Edinburgh
Culross, Robert	28	carpenter	Tayport
Cunningham, David	20	mason	23 Pitalpin Street, Lochee
Davidson, Thomas	28	farm servant	Linlathen
Dewar or Fowlis, Robert	21	mason	23 Pitalpin Street, Lochee
Easton, or Loudon, May Marion Montgomerie	53	widow	Galt Villa, Aberdeen
Graham, David	37	teacher	Stirling
Hamilton, John	32	grocer & spirit dealer	16 North Ellen Street
Henderson, James Foster	22	labourer	3 Church Street, Maxwelltown

Name	Age	Occupation	Address
Jack, William	23	grocer	57 Mains Road
Jobson, David	39	oil & colour merchant	3 Airlie Place
Johnston, David	24	railway guard	Edinburgh (Abbey Hill)
Johnston, George	25	mechanic	18 Beaconsfield Place, Victoria Road
Kinnear, Margaret	17	domestic servant	6 Shore Terrace
Lawson, John	25	plasterer	39 Lilybank Road
Leslie, James	22	clerk	Baffin Street
McBeth, David	44	railway guard	46 Castle Street
McDonald, David	11	schoolboy	70 Blackness Road
McDonald, William	41	sawmiller	70 Blackness Road
McIntosh, George	43	goods guard	25 Hawkhill
Mann or Hendry, Elizabeth	62	n/a	Prior Road, Forfar
Marshall, John	24	railway stoker	18 Hunter Street
Miller, James	26	flax dresser	Dysart
Milne, Elizabeth	21	dressmaker	High Street, Newburgh
Mitchell, David	37	engine driver	89 Peddie Street
Murdoch, James	21	engineer	1 Thistle Street
Murray, Donald	49	mail guard	13 South Ellen Street
Neish, David	37	teacher & registrar	51 Coupar Street, Lochee
Neish, Isabella Mary	5	daughter of above	51 Coupar Street, Lochee
Nelson, William	31	machine fitter	53 Monk St, Gateshead
Ness, George	21	railway stoker	Ogilvy Street, Tayport
Ness, Walter	24	saddler	4 Bain Square, Wellgate
Nicoll or McFarlane, Elizabeth	24	n/a	46 Bell Street
Peebles, James	15	apprentice grocer	Newport

Name	Age	Occupation	Address
Peebles, William	38	forester	Corriemoney, Inverness
Robertson, Alexander	23	labourer	100 Foundry Lane
Robertson, William	21	labourer	100 Foundry Lane
Salmond, Peter Greig	43	blacksmith	50 Princes Street
Scott, David	26	goods guard	7 Yeaman Shore
Scott, John	30	seaman	Tobias Street, Baltimore
Sharp, John	35	joiner	76 Commercial Street
Smart, Eliza	22	domestic servant	Union Mount, Perth Road
Spence, Annie	21	weaver	62 Kemback Street
Syme, Robert Frederick	22	clerk	Royal Hotel, Nethergate
Taylor, George	25	mason	56 Union Street, Maxwelltown
Threlfell, William	18	confectioner	9 Union Street, Maxwelltown
Veitch, William	18	cabinetmaker	39 Church Street
Watson, David	18	commission agent	Newport
Watson, David Livie	9	son of Robert Watson snr	12 Lawrence Street
Watson, Robert	6	son of Robert Watson snr	12 Lawrence Street
Watson, Robert	34	moulder	12 Lawrence Street

Source: Nicoll, M., Nicoll, C., Buttars, G., *Victims of the Tay Rail Bridge Disaster*, Tay Valley Family History Society, 2005

WILLIAM BROWN RECALLS THE DISASTER

(From the account in the Dundee City Archives. Brown was the grandson of Elizabeth Mann (62) and brother of Elizabeth Brown (14), both of whom were lost in the disaster.)

'Sunday night, December 28, 1879.

In the year 1879 I was then just a small boy. My age verging on 6 years of age. My father had died a year previous to this. My Mother being left a widow with a family of four – two boys and two girls. My eldest sister Elizabeth being 14 years and six months, my brother Alexander 10 years and my younger sister just a baby one year old. My elder sister's name was Elizabeth and my younger sister Jane Brown. My brother and sister Jane are this day still alive in Canada. We were not too well off, and at the time I am writing about we lived in the Arbroath Road Dundee to the west of Albert Street.

During the month of December 1879 my grandmother on my mother's side who lived in Forfar paid us a visit and after being with us for a week decided to pay her son Charles who lived in Leuchars a visit as well. I had been to Leuchars before and enjoyed every minute of it, and when I heard my grandmother had decided to take my sister Elizabeth and myself with her, Oh, I felt so very happy for the journey in the train across the Tay Bridge was still a happy memory. The morning of the day we were to leave for Leuchars arrived. And in my excitement I must have done something very wrong for my mother gave me a severe beating and I was locked in a room. What I had done, I cannot remember, but I must have felt I had been illused [sic] for in my anger I kicked the panel of the door in and got another beating and was then told I was not being allowed to go on the visit to Leuchars for being a such a bad boy and I then thought my heart was broken when I saw my grandmother and sister take their departure without me.

Well, the day arrived for their return and the weather in Dundee was terrible; a howling gale of wind and rain and I can remember the milkman had not turned up to deliver the milk and my mother was in a great state having no milk for her baby.

I was the only one in the house and was told by my mother I must go out and try to buy some milk so off I went on the errand which nearly caused me disaster once or twice, chimney cans flying through the air like pigeons and crashing in the streets. Shutters and windows blown in, it was a case of running up closes, every few feet I went. I escaped many near crashes but had to return home without the milk; I was very excited over my escapade and was sent to bed at once.

In the early morning a noise woke me up. I had been sleeping soundly all night after my night out, only it seemed someone was crying very loudly, so I rose in my nighty and crept to the top of the bedroom stairs and listened. Yes, someone was crying in the sitting room, so down I went slowly and listened at the door. Yes, I was right, someone was crying. I opened the door slowly and there I saw my uncle from Leuchars and my Mother and elder brother all in a terrible state of distress. My Mother crying as if her heart would break I ran over to Mother and asked her what was the matter. She certainly knew I was very fond of my sister who put me to bed every night. Her reply to me was in a broken voice. "Laddie you will never see your darling sister or your Grandmother again. The Tay Bridge has fallen down, taking the train with it, the train your Grandmother and sister were on, everybody in the train has been drowned."

For a while I could not grasp what I had been told. The Tay Bridge could never fall down it was too much for me to fathom so I went about all day in a dream, and when I was put to bed that night "and quietness to think" I then fully realised what a terrible disaster had happened. I did nothing else but cry all night, at the loss of one I loved so much, my dear sister Elisabeth.

Dundee that day was in a terrible state, what with the damage done by the gale and the great disaster to the Bridge and great sadness that none were saved to tell the tale.

Our early news was because of my Uncle deciding to accompany my Grandmother and sister in the train as far as Newport, then get the first train back to Leuchars. [This must be a mistake – the 'Edinburgh' did not stop at Newport. After so long an interval, it would not be surprising if William's memory of events in his early childhood had become unreliable.] The train on arrival at Newport my Uncle got out, waved goodbye and retired to the waiting room for the first train back home. Not long after he had made himself comfortable in his seat, he heard running about on the platform men, who were shouting to one another in the dark. He asked one man if anything was the matter. The reply was "Yes there is news given out that the Bridge has collapsed with that last train. We are going over to see if it is all true." My Uncle went along with them and found that it was all too true and the only thing left for him to do was to wait now for the first ferry boat to Dundee and inform my Mother of the terrible disaster, which he did that morning. Another rather sad thing happened shortly afterwards to my brother Alick. As everyone on board the train had perished, day after day bodies were being found on the beach as far down and further down than Broughty Ferry also carriages from the train washed up high and dry and lay there for quite a long time. But my brother felt determined to find his Grandmother and Sister so as soon as word came in that another body had been washed up, my brother went down to try to identify, but always no luck. In time he had seen so many bodies and in such fearful states of decomposure, his nerves went completely wrong and for two years afterwards that lad would never venture out of his house after darkness set in. However in due time his nerves fully recovered and he is still alive in Toronto, Canada, retired where he has been for the past 50 years. Also my sister (Jane) married name Aiken. My mother immigrated over there also and when she died many years ago she was the oldest lady in Toronto, 98 years. I myself am an old retired Ship Master and have had many adventures during my life at sea.

Yes these memories are always with me but so is the Tay Bridge disaster when December month comes along. I am now 76 years old and the date as I write this story is 30 November, year 1948, just 69 years since the disaster happened and my life was saved by being a naughty boy for which I thank God.'

BIBLIOGRAPHY

DOCUMENTARY SOURCES

Lamb Collection, Dundee Central Library
Kinnear Collection, Dundee University Library

Newspapers: *Dundee Advertiser*; *Dundee Courier*; *Edinburgh Courant*; *Fife Journal*; *Fife News*; *Glasgow Evening Times*; *Glasgow News*; *Graphic*; *Illustrated London News*; *Pall Mall Gazette*; *Perthshire Advertiser*; *Perthshire Constitutional*; *Railway Advocate*; *Railway News*; *Railway World*; *Scots Magazine*; *The Scotsman*; *The Times*

North British Railway Company, papers and correspondence; National Archives of Scotland
Papers re the Tay Bridge Exhibit of 1979; Dundee University Archives
Parliamentary Papers and Debates
Pattullo and Thornton Collection; Dundee City Archives
Thornton Collection; Dundee University Library
Valentine Collection; St Andrews University Archives
Washington Wilson Collection; Dundee Central Library

BOOKS AND ARTICLES

Barlow, C., 'The Tay Viaduct', *Proceedings of the Institution of Civil Engineers*, May, 1888, pp. 87–98
Barlow, C., *The New Tay Bridge* – a course of lectures at the Royal School of Military Engineering (London 1889)
Bidder, G.P., 'The Floating Railways across the Forth and Tay Ferries', *Proceedings of the Institution of Civil Engineers*, 1860–1, XX, p. 389
Bignall, V. (ed.), *The First Tay Bridge* (Hatfield, 1979)

Board of Trade Circular Letter, 10 July 1880, *Parliamentary Papers* 1880 LXIII (457)

Buchan, A., 'The Tay Bridge Storm of 28th December 1879', *Journal of Scottish Meteorological Society*, 1880, vol. 5, pp. 355–60

Davey, N., *The Tay Bridge Disaster* (Dundee, 1993)

Dow W.M., 'Destined for Disaster', *Scots Magazine*, December 1879, pp. 275–86

Dow W.M., 'Is this the Real Reason the Tay Bridge Fell?' *Dundee Courier and Advertiser*, 100th Anniversary Special, 1979

Drummond, B., 'The Story of the Tay Bridge', *Scots Magazine*, 1949, pp. 427–34

Duck, R.W., and Dow, W.M., 'Side–Scan Sonar reveals submerged remains of the First Tay Bridge', *Geoarcheology*, 1994, vol. 9, No. 2, pp. 139–53

Earnshaw, A., 'Sir Thomas Bouch, 1822–80, hero or villain?' 1989. Unpublished MS

Forrest, J. (ed.), *The Tay Viaduct* (London, 1888)

Gilkes, E., 'The Tay Bridge', *Proceedings of the Cleveland Institute of Engineers*, 1876, p. 12

Gren, André, *The Bridge is Down!* (Kettering, 2008)

Grothe, A., 'The Construction of the Tay Bridge', *Proceedings of the Edinburgh and Leith Engineers Society*, 1878

Hall, W., 'On the floating railways across the Forth and Tay ferries in connection with the Edinburgh, Dundee and Perth Railway', *Proceedings of the Institution of Civil Engineers*, 1861–2, XX

Hay, R., 'The Night the Bridge Fell', *Scots Magazine*, 1956, pp. 455–64

Hepburn, H.J., The Disaster that echoes down the years', *Scots Magazine*, 24 November, 1979

'Historic Accidents and Disasters', *The Engineer*, July 1941, pp. 18–20, 34–5

Hopkins, H.J., *A Span of Bridges: An Illustrated History* (Newton Abbot, 1970)

Inglis, W., 'The Construction of the Tay Viaduct', *Proceedings of the Institution of Civil Engineers*, 1888, pp. 99–132

Law, J.N.C., 'Sir Thomas Bouch – a scapegoat?' *Railway Magazine*, March 1965, p. 160; September, p. 537

Lewis, Peter, *Beautiful Railway Bridge of the Silvery Tay* (Stroud, 2004)

Lumley, R., *The Tay Bridge Disaster, the People's Story* (Stroud, 2013)

152

McGonagall, W., *Poetic Gems* (Dundee, 1989)

McKean, Charles, *Battle for the North* (London, 2006)

Martin, T.J., and McLeod, I.A., 'The Tay Bridge Disaster – a study in structural pathology', in Forth Rail Bridge Centenary Conference, *Developments in Structural Engineering*, 1995

Martin, T.J., and McLeod, I.A., 'The Tay Rail Bridge Disaster revisited', *Proceedings of the Institution of Civil Engineers, Bridge Engineering*, December 2004, 157, Issue BE4, pp. 187–192

Martin, T.J., *Tom Martin's Tay Bridge Disaster Web Pages*

'Memoir of Sir Thomas Bouch', *Institution of Civil Engineers*, 1881

Minute of Board of Trade, 15 July 1880, with Observations of Major–General Hutchinson. *Parliamentary Papers*, 1880 [c. 2624] LXIII 459

'On machinery and methods for founding the piers of the new Tay Bridge', *Engineering*, June, 1885

Nicoll, M., Nicoll, C., Buttars, G., *Victims of the Tay Rail Bridge Disaster*, Tay Valley Family History Society, 2005

Paxton, Roland A. (ed.), *100 Years of the Forth Bridge* (London, 1990)

Perkins, J., *The Tay Bridge Disaster* (Dundee, 1975)

Prebble, John, *The High Girders* (London, 1975 edition)

Report of the Committee of Inquiry into the Tay Bridge Disaster, with Proceedings and Minutes of Evidence, and Report of Mr Rothery. *Parliamentary Papers*, 1880 [c. 2616] XXXIX 1

Report of the Select Committee on the North Bridge Railway (Tay Bridge) Bill, with Proceedings and Minutes of Evidence. *Parliamentary Papers*, 1880 (311) XII 1

Robertson, C.J.A., 'The Cheap Railway Movement in Scotland', *Transport History*, 1974, VII, 1, pp. 1–40

Scotrail, *Tay Bridge Centenary* (Glasgow, 1987)

Shipway, J.S., *The Tay Railway Bridge, 1887–1987* (Edinburgh, 1987)

Simmons, J., *The Railways of Britain – a Historical Introduction* (London, 1961)

Smith, D.W., 'Bridge Failures', *Proceedings of the Institution of Civil Engineers*, August 1976, pp. 367–82

Smith, H.S., *The World's Great Bridges* (London, 1953)

'The New Tay Bridge', *Engineering*, June 1985

'The New Tay Viaduct', *Proceedings of the Institute of Mechanical Engineers*, August 1887

'The New Viaduct over the Tay', *The Engineer*, September 1885

'The Old and New Tay Bridges', *Railway Advocate*, November 1886

The Tay Bridge; its history and construction, with introduction and lithographs by Albert Grothe, John Leng & Co. (Dundee, 1878)

Tay Bridge Guide, John Leng & Co. (Dundee, 1887)

Thomas, J., *The Forgotten Railways of Scotland* (Newton Abbot, 1976)

Thomas, J., *The North British Railway* (Newton Abbot, 1969)

Thomas, J., *The Tay Bridge Disaster: New Light on the 1879 Tragedy* (Newton Abbot, 1972)

Walker, C., 'Bouch the Railway Builder', *Railway World*, May 1872

White I.N., *The Death Toll of the Tay Rail Bridge Disaster*, Newsletter of the North British Railway Studies Group, No. 122, 2014

NOTES

---

1. THE BRIDGE IS DOWN

1. For a discussion of number of victims of the Disaster, see Appendix 1.
2. Hepburn, H., 'The Disaster that Echoes down the Years', *Weekend Scotsman*, 24 November 1979.
3. *Report of the Committee of Inquiry into the Tay Bridge Disaster, Minutes of Evidence*, p. 31.
4. *Ibid.*, p. 26.
5. Rapley, J., *Sir Thomas Bouch – Builder of the Tay Bridge* (2007), p. 139.
6. *Ibid.*, pp. 23–4, 27, 34.
7. *Ibid.*, pp. 12, 14; *Dundee Courier*, 29 December 1879.
8. *Committee of Inquiry, Minutes of Evidence*, p. 13.
9. *Ibid.*, p. 21.
10. Thomas, J., *The Tay Bridge Disaster: New Light on the 1879 Tragedy* (1972), pp. 82–3, Prebble, John, *The High Girders* (1975), pp. 100–102 .
11. Thomas, J., *op. cit.*, p. 83; Prebble, J., *op. cit.*, p. 106.
12. *Committee of Inquiry, Minutes of Evidence*, pp. 3–4.
13. Prebble, J., *op. cit.*, pp.102–6.
14. *Committee of Inquiry, Minutes of Evidence*, pp. 5–6.
15. *Ibid.*, pp. 16–18.
16. *Ibid.*, pp. 18–19.
17. *Dundee Advertiser*, 29 December 1879.
18. *Committee of Inquiry, Minutes of Evidence*, pp. 15–16.
19. *Ibid.*, pp. 52–4; *Scotsman*, 30 December 1879.
20. Prebble, J., *op. cit.*, p. 97.
21. *Committee of Inquiry, Minutes of Evidence*, pp. 11–15; *Dundee Courier*, 29th December, 1879.
22. *Committee of Inquiry, Minutes of Evidence*, pp. 57–8.

23. *Ibid.*, pp. 4–9; *Scotsman*, 30 December 1879.

24. *Committee of Inquiry, Minutes of Evidence*, p. 34.

25. *Scotsman*, 30 December 1879; quoted in Drummond, B., 'The Story of the Tay Bridge', *Scots Magazine*, 1949, pp. 427–34.

26. *Dundee Advertiser*, Sunday 29 December 1879; *Scotsman*, 30 December 1879; Prebble, J., *op. cit.*, pp. 118–9.

27. James Smith to Mr Bell, Dundee University Archives (hereafter DUA), MS 30/8 (4).

28. For a discussion of the numbers of victims, see Appendix 1.

29. DUA MS 30/1 (4).

2. Railway Rivalry

30. *Herpath's Railway Journal*, 11 January 1851.

31. *Railway Times*, 3 April 1853.

32. Robertson, C.J.A., 'The Cheap Railway Movement in Scotland: the St Andrews Railway Company', *Transport History*, 1974, vii, 1, p. 7.

33. Thomas, J., *The North British Railway*, vol. 1 (1969), p. 217; *Tay Bridge Disaster*, p. 21.

34. Prebble, J., *op. cit.*, p. 24.

35. 'Sir Thomas Bouch', *Proceedings of the Institute of Civil Engineers*, vol. 63 (1881), pp. 301ff; *Dictionary of National Biography*; DUA MS 30/1 (20b) – obituaries of Sir Thomas Bouch.

36. *Proceedings of the Institute of Civil Engineers*, vol. 20, pp. 376–90; Thomas, J., *Tay Bridge Disaster*, p. 18; Paxton, R.A., *100 years of the Forth Bridge* (1990), pp. 24–6; Bidder, G.P., 'The Floating Railways across the Forth and Tay Ferries', and Hall, W., 'On the Floating Railways across the Forth and Tay Ferries, in connection with the Edinburgh, Perth and Dundee Railway.' *Proceedings of the Institute of Civil Engineers*, 1861–2, XX, *passim*.

37. DUA MS 30/1 (25c) – obituary of Thomas Bouch.

38. Quoted in Thomas, J., *Tay Bridge Disaster*, p. 18.

39. *Ibid.*, p. 19; Paxton, R.A., *op. cit.*, p. 24.

40. Walker, C., 'Bouch the Railway Builder', *Railway World*, 1972, 'The Centenary of Hownes Gill Viaduct', *British Railway Journal*, NE Region, vol. 9 (5), May 1938, pp. 126–7; DUA MS 30/1 (10); MS 30/1 (12) .

41. DUA MS 30/1 (9); MS 30/1 (12).

42. DUA MS 30/2 (2).
43. Robertson, C.J.A., *op. cit.*, pp. 1–39.
44. Ibid., p. 17; Scottish Record Office, BR/SNR/1/2, *St Andrews Railway Minutes*, 24 March 1865.
45. Dundee Public Libraries, *Lamb Collection* (hereafter LC), 303 (1), MS note on Tay Bridge, 10 July 1818.
46. LC 303 (10) – The Tay Bridge Disaster; John Leng & Co., *The History and Construction of the Tay Bridge* (1878) p. 11.
47. Thomas, J., *North British Railway*, vol. 1, p. 218; for a full account of Bouch's plan for the Forth Bridge, see Paxton, R.A., *100 Years*, Ch. 1.
48. LC 303 (2) – *Dundee Advertiser*, 18 October 1864; Leng & Co., *History and Construction*, pp. 14–15; Prebble, J., *op. cit.*, pp. 28–30.
49. Rapley, J., *Thomas Bouch, the Builder of the Tay Bridge*, p.117.
50. Leng & Co., *History and Construction*, pp. 16–7; *Minute of agreement between the North British Railway Company and the Provost and Town Council of Perth*, 21 March 1870, National Archives of Scotland, NBR 3/9.
51. LC 303 (2) – Meetings re Tay Bridge Plan, 1869–70.
52. Leng & Co., *History and Construction*, p. 21.
53. *Ibid.*, pp. 31–2.
54. LC 303 (10); Thomas, J., *Tay Bridge Disaster*, pp. 23–5; Prebble, J., *op. cit.*, p. 32.
55. Leng & Co., *History and Construction*, p. 37.
56. LC 303 (10); Thomas, J., *Tay Bridge Disaster*, p. 25; Prebble, J., *op. cit.*, pp. 35–8.
57. Leng & Co., *History and Construction*, pp. 37–8.
58. *Ibid.*, pp. 39–40.
59. LC 303 (1A) – Patrick Matthew correspondence; Prebble, J., *op. cit.*, pp. 37–8.

3. The Bridge Takes Shape

60. LC 303 (3); Prebble, J., *op. cit.*, p. 16, 35–6.
61. LC 303 (10); DUA MS 30/1; Thomas, J., *Tay Bridge Disaster*, pp. 29–30.
62. *Dundee Advertiser*, 26 September 1871. The articles advocating a double line were written personally by the proprietor, John Leng.

63. Reprinted in the *Dundee Courier*, 18 April 1872.
64. *Dundee Advertiser*, 22 July 1872; Leng & Co., *History and Construction*, pp. 52–3; Thomas, J., *Tay Bridge Disaster*, pp. 25, 30–4; Prebble, J., *op. cit.*, pp. 39–41.
65. Thomas, J., *Tay Bridge Disaster*, pp. 40–1.
66. Leng & Co., *History and Construction*, pp. 52–3.
67. LC 303 (4).
68. The method of construction was explained in a series of four public lectures given in Dundee in March 1873 by Albert Grothe. LC 303 (4); Leng & Co., *History and Construction*, pp. 54–7.
69. *Dundee Advertiser*, 26 June 1871.
70. LC 303 (4).
71. Leng & Co., *History and Construction*, p. 68; *Dundee Advertiser*, 27 August 1873; Prebble, J., *op. cit.*, pp. 55–7.
72. Leng & Co., *History and Construction*, pp. 68–70; Prebble, J., *op. cit.*, pp. 54, 59–64; Thomas, J., *Tay Bridge Disaster*, pp. 53–4, 56–8.
73. LC 303 (5); Prebble, J., *op. cit.*, p. 45; Thomas, J., *Tay Bridge Disaster*, p. 39.
74. Leng & Co., *History and Construction*, pp. 58–9.
75. Lewis, P., *Beautiful Railway Bridge of the Silvery Tay*, p. 32.
76. Thomas, J., *Tay Bridge Disaster*, p. 39.
77. *Ibid.*; *Committee of Inquiry, Minutes of Evidence*, p. 180.
78. Thomas,, J., *Tay Bridge Disaster*, pp. 48–9; see for example the testimony of Frank Beattie in defence of the Wormit foundry, and criticism of it by Henry Law, *Committee of Inquiry, Minutes of Evidence*, pp. 180, 241ff.
79. Gilkes to Wieland, 26 May 1877, quoted in Thomas, J., *Tay Bridge Disaster*, pp. 58–9.
80. *The Times*, 7 January 1876.
81. *Dundee Advertiser*, 1 September 1877; Leng & Co., *History and Construction*, p. 73.
82. There is no record of Grant's actual words – this comment is put into his mouth by John Prebble (*op. cit.*, p. 52). According to the report in the *Advertiser*, Grant merely remarked on 'the singularly substantial character of the work.' *Dundee Advertiser*, 1 September 1877.

4. The Tay Is Bridged

83. McGonagall, W., 'The Railway Bridge of the Silvery Tay'.

84. Quoted in Hamilton, A., 'The Tay Bridge Disaster', *The Times*, 1 December 1979.

85. Rapley, J., *op. cit.*, p. 129.

86. *Dundee Advertiser*, 25 September 1877.

87. Barlow, W.H., to Roddick, R.D., 1 October 1877, DUA MS 30/8.

88. Quoted in Prebble, J., *op. cit.*, pp. 70–1; Thomas, J., *Tay Bridge Disaster*, p. 63.

89. *Committee of Inquiry, Minutes of Evidence*, p. 378.

90. Leng & Co., *History and Construction*, pp. 90–111; Thomas, J., *Tay Bridge Disaster*, pp. 63–4; Prebble, J., *op. cit.*, pp. 77–82.

91. Select Committee on the North British Railway (Tay Bridge) Bill, 1880, p. 3; Thomas, J., *Tay Bridge Disaster*, p. 65; Prebble, J., *op. cit.*, pp. 84–5.

92. Prebble, J., *op. cit.*, pp. 85–9.

93. *Pattullo and Thornton Collection*, Dundee City Archives. GD/TD 1 6/24, 26.

94. *Committee of Inquiry, Appendix*, p. xli.

95. Rapley, J., *op. cit.*, p. 130.

96. *Ibid.*; Thomas, J., *Tay Bridge Disaster*, p. 79.

5. After the Fall

97. DUA MS 30/2 (1).

98. *The Times*, 29 December 1879.

99. Quoted in Thomas, J., *Tay Bridge Disaster*, p. 106.

100. *Dundee Courier*, n.d. January 1880, LC 303.

101. For a full account of the search and diving operations, see Prebble, J., *op. cit.* pp. 125–37.

102. LC 303 (13, 14); *Edinburgh Courant*, 31 December 1880; Prebble, J., *op. cit.*, p. 127.

103. *Committee of Inquiry, Minutes of Evidence*, pp. 38–48; Prebble, J., *op. cit.*, p.127. There is some confusion over the name of the diver, John Cox or Fox. He appears as Cox in the Minutes of Evidence, but as Fox in all the newspaper reports.

104. Prebble, J., *op. cit.*, p. 131.

105. *Ibid*, pp. 152–5.
106. *Dundee Advertiser*, 15 January 1880, LC 303 (14).
107. *Committee of Inquiry, Minutes of Evidence*, p. 39; Thomas, J., *Tay Bridge Disaster*, pp. 147–50.
108. *Committee of Inquiry, Minutes of Evidence*, pp. 38–49; Thomas, J., *Tay Bridge Disaster*, pp. 112–4.
109. LC 303 (16) p. 5; Prebble, J., *op. cit.*, p.137.
110. Dundee City Archives, CD/TD 1/21/9.
111. *Ibid.*, GD/TD/ 1/21/2, 4, 8; Prebble, J., *op. cit.*, p. 152.
112. Unidentified newspaper, December 1880, LC 304 (1).
113. *Railway Observer*, November 1988, p. 549; Unidentified newspaper, March 1881, LC 303 (16) p. 27; *The Times*, 30 December 1880.
114. Report of Dugald Drummond to Board of NBR, 17 September 1880. BR/NBR/10/8. While the engine proved to be salvageable, the carriages were too badly damaged to be returned to service, and the wood from them was commonly made into mementoes of the disaster. A wooden knife carved from a piece of a carriage used to be on display in the Ferry Inn in Broughty Ferry (the Ferry Inn is now a tapas bar – the Sol Y Sombra – but the knife is still in the possession of the proprietors, the Stewart family). Three walking sticks made from the same material were presented to the off–duty driver, guard and fireman, who should have been travelling in the train, but missed it through overstaying their time in a local pub. *Railway Magazine*, October 1875, p. 515.

6. Court of Inquiry

115. *Report of the Committee of Inquiry into the Tay Bridge Disaster, and Report of Mr Rothery*, pp. 2–3; Thomas, J., *Tay Bridge Disaster*, p. 110.
116. *Report*, pp. 3–55.
117. Precognition of David Young, *Thornton Collection*, DUA MS 17/7/2; Precognition of James Edward, *Pattullo and Thornton Collection*, Dundee City Archives GD/TD/ 1 6/24.
118. Precognition of W.B. Thomson, *Ibid.*, GD/TD 1 20/91.
119. Precognition of Robertson, Whitehurst, *Ibid.*, GD/TD 1 18/81, 20/92: Thomas, J., *Tay Bridge Disaster* p. 124.

120. *Committee of Inquiry, Minutes of Evidence*, pp. 57–65, 85–7, 193–4.
121. *Ibid.*, pp. 144–52.
122. *Ibid.*, pp. 158–80.
123. *Ibid.*, pp. 215–25.
124. *Ibid*, p. 303.
125. *Ibid.*, pp. 379–95.
126. *Ibid.*, pp. 385–91, 391–97.
127. *Ibid.*, pp. 398–420.
128. William Pole and Allan D. Stewart to Sir Thomas Bouch, 25 February 1880, BR/NBR/10/8.
129. *Report of Committee of Inquiry*, pp. 10–15.
130. *Report of Mr Rothery*, pp. 15–48.

7. THE REASON WHY

131. E. Dean to Board of Trade, 1 January 1880; W.E. Surtees to Rothery, 7 January 1880; E. Talbot to Lord Sandon, 30 December 1879; James Murray to Board of Trade, 10 January 1880, BR/NBR/10/8.
132. A.J. Dickson to Adam Johnstone, telegram, 14 April 1880, BR/NBR/10/9.
133. Report of Dugald Drummond to North British Railway Board, 17 September 1880, BR/NBR/10/8.
134. Houston, S., 'Thoughts on the Tay Bridge Disaster', DUA MS 30/1; LC 303 (13); LC 303 (16).
135. Thomas, J., *Tay Bridge Disaster*, pp. 199–201; Dow, D.W., 'Destined for Disaster', *Scots Magazine*, December 1989, pp. 280–82.
136. Unidentified newspaper, L C 303 (11).
137. McKean, C., *Battle for the North* (London, 2006), p. 5.
138. Lumley, R., *The Tay Bridge Disaster – The People's Story*, p. 176.
139. *Scotsman*, n.d., L C 303 (11).
140. Report of James Brunlees to Adam Johnstone, 14 April 1880, BR/NBR/10/8.
141. Unidentified newspaper cutting, L C 303(12).
142. Smith, D.W., 'Bridge Failures', *Proceedings of the Institute of Civil Engineers*, August 1876, pp. 367ff.; Martin, T.J., and Macleod, I.A., 'The Tay Bridge Disaster: a study in structural pathology',

in Forth Rail Bridge Centenary Conference, *Developments in Structural Engineering*, 1993, pp. 6–8.

143. William Pole and Allan D. Stewart to Sir Thomas Bouch, 25 February 1880, BR/NBR/10/10/41. *Committee of Inquiry, Minutes of Evidence*, pp. 180, 248, 249, 481, 523; Telephone interview with William Dow; according to Martin and Macleod, *Tay Bridge Disaster* p. 6, in the tests it was the cast-iron lugs which failed in every case but one.

144. Lewis, P.R., and Reynolds, K., 'Forensic Engineering: a reapprais- al of the Tay Bridge Disaster', *Interdisciplinary Science Reviews*, 2002, vol. 27, No. 4, pp. 287–98; Lewis, P.R., *Beautiful Railway Bridge of the Silvery Tay*, (Stroud, 2004).

145. Lewis, P.R., and Reynolds, K., 'Forensic engineering: a reappraisal of the Tay Bridge Disaster', *Interdisciplinary Science Reviews*, 2002, vol. 27, No. 4, pp. 287–98.

146. Rapley, J., *op. cit.*, p. 125.

147. Martin, T., and McLeod, I.A., 'The Tay Rail Bridge disaster – a reappraisal based on modern analysis methods', *Proceedings of the Institution of Civil Engineers, Civil Engineering*, 1995, 108, May, pp. 77–83; 'The Tay Rail Bridge disaster revisited', *Proceedings of the Institution of Civil Engineers, Bridge Engineering*, December 2004, 157, Issue BE4, pp. 187–192. See also *Tom Martin's Tay Bridge Disaster Web Pages*, www.taybridgedisaster. co.uk.

148. Lewis, P.R., *Beautiful Railway Bridge of the Silvery Tay* (Stroud, 2004), pp. 102–3.

149. William Pole and Allan D. Stewart to Sir Thomas Bouch, 25 February 1880, BR/NBR/10/10/41.

150. *Committee of Inquiry, Minutes of Evidence*, p. 400, (Sir) T. Bouch to Col. Yolland, 6 October 1869; Col. Yolland to Bouch, 9 October 1869.

151. *Scotsman*, 15 July 1880.

152. Thomas, J., *The Forgotten Railways of Scotland* (1976), DUA MS 30/1 (5).

153. Thomas, J., *Tay Bridge Disaster*, p. 195; L C 303 (16).

154. *Observations of Major–General Hutchinson*, 12 July 1880. *Parliamentary Papers*, 1880 [c.2642] LXXX 459. Hutchinson offered a very similar excuse to the Court of Inquiry. See *Committee of Inquiry, Minutes of Evidence*, p. 376.

155. *Minute of the Board of Trade*, 15 July 1880. *Parliamentary Papers*, 1880 [c.2642] LXXX 459.

156. *Report of the Court of Inquiry*, pp. 35–6.

157. MacLeod, I.A., Martin, T., Paxton, R.A., to author, 23 March 2015.

158. *Ibid*.

159. George Wieland to Adam Johnstone, 14 May 1880, BR/NBR/10/10/ 14.

160. *Parliamentary Debates*, House of Lords, 2 July 1880; Thomas, J., *Tay Bridge Disaster*, pp. 177–79.

161. The terms of Dickson's correspondence with Yolland and Barlow were recorded in letters he wrote to Adam Johnstone on 5, 14 and 16 July 1880, BR/NBR/10/10/23, 25, 31.

162. Wieland to Johnstone, 7 July 1880, BR/NBR/10/10/26; Stirling to Johnstone, 8 July 1880, BR/NBR/10/10/27.

163. *Parliamentary Debates*, House of Commons, 7 July 1880; Walker to Johnstone, 8 July 1880, BR/NBR/10/10/28; Bouch to Johnstone, 14 July 1880, BR/NBR/10/10/32.

164. Earnshaw, 'Bouch', pp. 17–8; *Dictionary of National Biography*; Thomas, J., *Tay Bridge Disaster*, p. 193.

8. FROM THE ASHES OF THE OLD

165. *Scotsman*, 30 December 1879; L C 303 (12) pp. 17, 29, 31.

166. *Perthshire Constitutional*, 21 January 1880; *Perthshire Advertiser*, 21 January 1880; *Dundee Advertiser*, 7 May 1880.

167. *Report of Select Committee into North British Railway Bill*, 1880, p. x; Barlow, C., 'The Tay Viaduct, Dundee', pp. 87–8.

168. Barlow, 'Tay Viaduct', pp. 88–9; Shipway, J.S., *The Tay Railway Bridge, 1889–1987* (1987), pp. 12–3.

169. Barlow, 'Tay Viaduct', p. 129.

170. Shipway, *Tay Railway Bridge*, pp. 15–6.

171. Barlow, 'Tay Viaduct', pp. 91–2.

172. Unidentified newspaper cutting, December 1881, L C 304 (1); Shipway, *Tay Rail Bridge*, pp. 30–1; 44 and 45 Vict. c. cxxxviii – An Act to provide for the restoration of the Railway communications across the Tay, near Dundee, and for other purposes.

173. Barlow, 'Tay Viaduct', pp. 91–2.

174. Inglis, W., 'The construction of the Tay Viaduct', pp. 100–2; unidentified newspaper cutting, L C 304 (1).
175. *Pall Mall Gazette*, 5 December 1885. L C 304 (1).
176. Barlow, 'Tay Viaduct', pp. 93–4; Shipway, *Tay Railway Bridge*, pp. 16–8; Inglis, 'Construction', pp. 100–15. At some point after the completion of the new bridge in 1887, the old brick piers were demolished above the water line and allowed to fall on to the river bed. Their positions were rediscovered in 1994 using sonar scanning equipment. Duck, R.W., and Dow, W.M., 'Side-Scan Sonar reveals remains of the first Tay Bridge', *Geoarcheology*, 1994, vol. 9, No. 2, pp. 139–53.
177. *The Times*, 26 September 1883.
178. Unidentified newspaper cutting, 2 February 1884, L C 304 (2).
179. Unidentified newspaper cutting, 17 May 1884, L C 304 (1).
180. Unidentified newspaper cutting, 5 January 1885, L C 304 (5); *Dundee Advertiser*, 28 September 1885.
181. Unidentified newspaper cutting, 16 June 1886, L C 304 (5).
182. *Dundee Advertiser*, 20 June 1887; unidentified newspaper cutting, June 1887, L C 304 (4).
183. McGonagall, W., *Poetic Gems.*

INDEX